National Education Policy (NEP), 2020 and the Role of Teachers

National Education Policy (NEP), 2020 and the Role of Teachers

By

Nishi Tyagi

Assistant Professor, School of Education,
Sharda University, Greater Noida

and

Akanksha Srivastava

Associate Professor, School of Education,
Sharda University, Greater Noida

New Century Publications
New Delhi, India

NEW CENTURY PUBLICATIONS,
74, Ansari Road, Ground Floor,
Daryaganj, New Delhi – 110 002 (India)

Tel.: 011- 4358 7398, 4101 7798, 2324 7798
E-mail: info@newcenturypublications.com

www.newcenturypublications.com

Editorial office:
4800/24, Ansari Road,
Daryaganj, New Delhi – 110 002

Tel.: 98117 88655

Copyright © 2021 by authors

All rights reserved. No part of this book may be reproduced, stored in a retrieval system, or transmitted in any form or by any means, mechanical, photocopying, recording, or otherwise without the prior written permission of the publisher.

First Published: **2021**

ISBN: **978-81-7708-519-8**

Published by New Century Publications and printed at Milan Enterprises, New Delhi

Designs: Patch Creative Unit, New Delhi

PRINTED IN INDIA

About the Book

Education is one of the major *life-processes* of human beings. Just as there are certain indispensable vital processes of life in the biological sense, so also education may be considered a vital process in a social sense. Education is indispensable to normal living. Without education, the individual would be unqualified for meaningful existence.

Education is essential for everyone. It is the level of education that helps people earn respect and recognition. It is a vital part of life both personally and socially. Education is fundamental for achieving full human potential, developing an equitable and just society, and promoting national development. Providing universal access to quality education is the key to India's continued ascent, and leadership on the global stage in terms of economic growth, social justice and equality, and national integration.

Teachers are an extremely important aspect of any society for a number of reasons. Teachers educate the youth of society who, in turn, become the leaders of the next generation of people. Teachers, through teaching, mould the minds of children and young people in their most impressionable years of life. Things which students learn from their teachers are most likely to stay with them, in one form or the other, for the rest of their lives.

National Education Policy (NEP), 2020 is the first education policy of the 21st century and aims to address the many growing developmental imperatives of India. NEP, 2020 lays particular emphasis on the development of the creative potential of each individual. It is based on the principle that education must develop not only cognitive capacities but also social, ethical, and emotional capacities and dispositions.

This book explains and examines various aspects of education system at different levels with special reference to India. It particularly focuses on the role and attitude of teachers in imparting economically and socially relevant education. A case study in this regard also forms part of the book.

About the Authors

Dr. Nishi Tyagi is currently Assistant Professor, School of Education, Sharda University. With a Ph.D. degree in Education and Sanskrit Literature from CCS University, Meerut, she has a diverse academic and professional career spanning 15 years. She has contributed to the Development of Handbook for Teachers Working in Special Training Centres, Department of Elementary Education, NCERT, New Delhi. She has extensive experience of designing curriculum and conducting professional development programmes on teacher education at national and international levels. She has authored and edited several books and published numerous research papers in reputed journals on multi-dimensional issues on education. Her research interests include educational management, language education, teacher education, and psychology of education.

Dr. Akanksha Srivastava is presently Associate Professor, School of Education, Sharda University, Greater Noida. Apart from a Doctorate in Education from Nagpur University, she also holds M.A. degrees in Education and English, and M.Sc. in Anthropology. She has been a part of teaching profession for many years and worked at Universities in Dehradun, Jammu and Nagpur. Her works have been presented and published in the form of papers in various journals. She has delivered many invited lectures and acted as resource person in various workshops and conferences. Her fields of interest include educational psychology and public communication.

Contents

About the Book .... *v*
About the Authors .... *vi*
Preface .... *xi-xii*

1. Main Provisions of National Education Policy (NEP), 2020
1-26

1.1 Introduction
1.2 Fundamental Principles of NEP, 2020
1.3 Vision of NEP, 2020
1.4 School Education
1.5 Higher Education
1.6 Other Key Areas of Focus
1.7 Implementation of NEP, 2020

2. Education and the Role of Teachers
27-35

2.1 Why Education is Essential?
2.2 Education and Development
2.3 Teachers as Catalysts of the Society
2.4 Qualities of a Good Teacher
2.5 Teacher-Student Relationship

3. Education and Socio-economic Development
36-42

3.1 Human Resources and Development
3.2 Objectives of Education
3.3 Education and Social Development
3.4 Education and Economic Development
3.5 Manpower Planning
3.6 Public-Private-Partnership in Education

4. Studies Related to Attitude of Teachers towards Teaching: A Review
43-55

4.1 Studies Conducted in India
4.2 Studies Conducted Abroad

viii National Education Policy (NEP), 2020 and the Role of Teachers

4.3 Reflections on Various Studies

5. Attitude of Teachers towards Teaching   56-70
5.1 Significance of Attitude of Teachers
5.2 Components of Attitude
5.3 Characteristics of Attitude
5.4 Attitude Formation
5.5 Theories of Attitude Formation
5.6 Teacher Training and Attitudes

6. Attitude of Prospective Teachers towards Teaching Profession: A Research-based Case Study   71-84
6.1 Teacher as a Dynamic Force of an Institution
6.2 Behaviour of Teacher in the Classroom
6.3 Dissatisfied Teachers
6.4 Major Findings of the Study
6.5 Conclusions
6.6 Educational Implications
6.7 Suggestions for Further Research

7. Education, Women Empowerment and Literacy Rates   85-105
7.1 Education and Human Potential
7.2 Education in Ancient India
7.3 Constitutional Provisions Regarding Education
7.4 Role of Education in the Development Process
7.5 Objectives of Education Policy
7.6 Education and Women Empowerment
7.7 Women in Decision-making
7.8 Trends in Literacy Rates
7.9 Promotion of Indian Languages, Arts, and Culture
7.10 Recruitment and Deployment of Teachers

Contents

ix

8. Elementary Education   **106-113**
8.1 Elementary Education Policy
8.2 Select Programmes for Elementary Education
8.3 Problem Areas in Elementary Education

9. Secondary and Vocational Education   **114-129**
9.1 Secondary Education
9.2 Vocational Education

10. Higher and Technical Education   **130-151**
10.1 Higher Education
10.2 Technical Education
10.3 Medical Education
10.4 Areas of Concern
10.5 National Education Policy (NEP), 2020 on
    Higher Education

11. Education and Skill Development   **152-173**
11.1 Meaning and Importance of Skill
    Development
11.2 Job-relevant Skills
11.3 On-the-job Training (OJT)
11.4 Matching Supply of Skills with Demand
11.5 System of Skill Development in India
11.6 Special Target Groups for Skill
    Development
11.7 Skill Development for Women Workers
11.8 National Policy for Skill Development and
    Entrepreneurship (NPSDE), 2015
11.9 National Skill Development Mission
    (NSDM), 2015
11.10 Pradhan Mantri Kaushal Vikas Yojana
    PMKVY)
11.11 National Apprenticeship Training Scheme
    (NATS)

x   National Education Policy (NEP), 2020 and the Role of Teachers

12. Adult Education   **174-181**
12.1 National Literacy Mission (NLM)
12.2 Total Literacy Campaign (TLC)
12.3 Jan Shikshan Sansthan (JSS)
12.4 Saakshar Bharat
12.5 Weaknesses of Adult Education Programmes
12.6 Twelfth Five Year Plan (2012-17) on Adult
    Education
12.7 National Education Policy (NEP), 2020 on
    Adult Education and Lifelong Learning

13. Internet and Education   **182-192**
13.1 Major Uses of Internet
13.2 Internet and Students
13.3 Collaborative Teaching
13.4 Newspaper Reading
13.5 Internet for Research and Academics
13.6 Negative Aspects
13.7 National Education Policy (NEP), 2020 on
    Online and Digital Education

Bibliography   **193-206**
Index   **207-214**

Preface

Since the dawn of Independence in 1947, efforts are being made in India to raise the standard of living of the masses. The success of such efforts, along with other factors, depends to a great extent on the quality of manpower which, in turn, is influenced by the standard of education in the country. India's future depends on the quantity and quality of education.

Through education, man tries to seek new ideas and new ways of life. It is again through education that he promotes his intelligence and adds to his knowledge to move in the world for good or evil. Thus, he attempts to understand himself in relation to the world around him and to transmit the knowledge gained to the succeeding generations. His life in the complex world is governed not only by the biological process, but also by a social process.

Education is one of the major *life-processes* of human beings. Just as there are certain indispensable vital processes of life in the biological sense, so also education may be considered a vital process in a social sense. Education is indispensable to normal living. Without education, the individual would be unqualified for meaningful existence.

Education is essential for everyone. It is the level of education that helps people earn respect and recognition. It is a vital part of life both personally and socially.

The importance of education for the development of a country must not be underestimated because education is the tool which alone can inculcate national and cultural values and liberate people from false prejudice, ignorance and representations. Education provides the required knowledge, technique, skill and information and enables us to understand the rights and duties towards our family, society and the motherland at large. Education expands our vision and outlook, provokes the spirit of healthy competition and a desire to fight ignorance, injustice, corruption, violence, disparity and communalism, the greatest hazards to the progress of the nation.

Without education, life would be disastrous and detrimental. Consequently, governments around the world are trying their best to make education universal and accessible for everyone, particularly the poor and the disabled. There are still regions and places where the inhabitants are uneducated and unaware of what is happening in the world, in the country and in their region.

A profession is important for individuals to carry on their life and for their happiness. It also indirectly affects one's lifestyle, social prestige and economic status. A profession also has a vital role in satisfying one's psycho-social needs. Those who have chosen teaching as a profession should possess the necessary abilities and capabilities to do justice to their choice.

Teachers are an extremely important aspect of any society for a number of reasons. Teachers educate the youth of society who, in turn, become the leaders of the next generation of people. Teachers, through teaching, mould the minds of children and young people in their most impressionable years of life. Things which students learn from their teachers are most likely to stay with them, in one form or the other, for the rest of their lives. Hence, teachers certainly have a significant mark on the development of young minds who, if properly trained, can be responsible and productive members of the society.

Teachers are the key factor of an education system. Besides being equipped with universal culture and professional knowledge, teachers are also expected to have positive attitude towards their profession. A positive attitude is essential to maintain a healthy classroom environment.

National Education Policy, 2020 has accorded prime of place to teachers who shape the future of our children and, therefore, the future of our nation.

NOIDA

Nishi Tyagi
Akanksha Srivastava

1

Main Provisions of National Education Policy (NEP), 2020

National Education Policy, 2020 is the first education policy of the 21st century and aims to address the many growing developmental imperatives of India. NEP, 2020 proposes the revision and revamping of all aspects of the education structure, including its regulation and governance, to create a new system that is aligned with the aspirational goals of 21st century education, while building upon India's traditions and value systems. NEP, 2020 lays particular emphasis on the development of the creative potential of each individual. It is based on the principle that education must develop not only cognitive capacities but also social, ethical, and emotional capacities and dispositions. Main provisions of NEP, 2020 are detailed below.

1.1 Introduction

Education is fundamental for achieving full human potential, developing an equitable and just society, and promoting national development. Providing universal access to quality education is the key to India's continued ascent, and leadership on the global stage in terms of economic growth, social justice and equality, scientific advancement, national integration, and cultural preservation. Universal high-quality education is the best way forward for developing and maximizing our country's rich talents and resources for the good of the individual, the society, the country, and the world. India will have the highest population of young people in the world over the next decade, and our ability to provide high-quality educational opportunities to them will determine the future of our country.

2 National Education Policy (NEP), 2020 and the Role of Teachers

The global education development agenda reflected in Goal 4 (SDG 4) of the 2030 Agenda for Sustainable Development, adopted by India in 2015, seeks to "ensure inclusive and equitable quality education and promote lifelong learning opportunities for all" by 2030. Such a lofty goal will require the entire education system to be reconfigured to support and foster learning, so that all of the critical targets and goals of the 2030 Agenda for Sustainable Development can be achieved.

The world is undergoing rapid changes in the knowledge landscape. With various dramatic scientific and technological advances, such as the rise of big data, machine learning, and artificial intelligence, many unskilled jobs worldwide may be taken over by machines, while the need for a skilled workforce, particularly involving mathematics, computer science, and data science, in conjunction with multidisciplinary abilities across the sciences, social sciences, and humanities, will be increasingly in greater demand. With climate change, increasing pollution, and depleting natural resources, there will be a sizeable shift in how we meet the world's energy, water, food, and sanitation needs, again resulting in the need for new skilled labour, particularly in biology, chemistry, physics, agriculture, climate science, and social science. The growing emergence of epidemics and pandemics will also call for collaborative research in infectious disease management and development of vaccines and the resultant social issues heightens the need for multidisciplinary learning. There will be a growing demand for humanities and art, as India moves towards becoming a developed country as well as among the three largest economies in the world.

Indeed, with the quickly changing employment landscape and global ecosystem, it is becoming increasingly critical that children not only learn, but more importantly learn how to learn. Education thus, must move towards less content, and more towards learning about how to think critically and solve problems, how to be creative and multidisciplinary, and how to innovate, adapt, and absorb new material in novel and changing fields. Pedagogy must evolve to make education more experiential, holistic, integrated, inquiry-driven, discovery-oriented, learner-centred, discussion-based, flexible, and, of course, enjoyable. The curriculum must include basic arts, crafts, humanities, games, sports and fitness, languages, literature, culture, and values, in addition to science and mathematics, to develop all aspects and capabilities of learners; and make education more well-rounded, useful, and fulfilling to the learner. Education must build character, enable learners to be ethical, rational, compassionate, and caring, while at the same time prepare them for gainful, fulfilling employment.

The gap between the current state of learning outcomes and what is required must be bridged through undertaking major reforms that bring the highest quality, equity, and integrity into the system, from early childhood care and education through higher education. The aim must be for India to have an education system by 2040 that is second to none, with equitable access to the highest-quality education for all learners regardless of social or economic background.

The new education policy must provide to all students, irrespective of their place of residence, a quality education system, with particular focus on historically marginalized, disadvantaged, and underrepresented groups. Education is a great leveller and is the best tool for achieving economic and social mobility, inclusion, and equality. Initiatives must be in place to ensure that all students from such groups, despite inherent obstacles, are provided various targeted opportunities to enter and excel in the educational system.

These elements must be incorporated taking into account the local and global needs of the country and with a respect for and deference to its rich diversity and culture. Instilling knowledge of India and its varied social, cultural, and technological needs, its inimitable artistic, language, and knowledge traditions, and its strong ethics in India's young people is considered critical for purposes of national pride, self-confidence, self-knowledge, cooperation, and integration.

4   National Education Policy (NEP), 2020 and the Role of Teachers

The purpose of the education system is to develop good human beings capable of rational thought and action, possessing compassion and empathy, courage and resilience, scientific temper and creative imagination, with sound ethical moorings and values. It aims at producing engaged, productive, and contributing citizens for building an equitable, inclusive, and plural society as envisaged by our Constitution.

A good education institution is one in which every student feels welcomed and cared for, where a safe and stimulating learning environment exists, where a wide range of learning experiences are offered, and where good physical infrastructure and appropriate resources conducive to learning are available to all students. Attaining these qualities must be the goal of every educational institution. However, at the same time, there must also be seamless integration and coordination across institutions and across all stages of education.

1.2 Fundamental Principles of NEP, 2020

The fundamental principles that will guide both the education system at large, as well as the individual institutions within it are as under:

1. Recognizing, identifying, and fostering the unique capabilities of each student, by sensitizing teachers as well as parents to promote each student's holistic development in both academic and non-academic spheres.

2. According the highest priority to achieving foundational literacy and numeracy by all students by grade 3.

3. Flexibility, so that learners have the ability to choose their learning trajectories and programmes, and thereby choose their own paths in life according to their talents and interests.

4. No hard separations between arts and sciences, between curricular and extra-curricular activities, between vocational and academic streams, etc. in order to eliminate harmful hierarchies among, and silos between different areas of learning.

Main Provisions of National Education Policy (NEP), 2020

5. Multi-disciplinarity and a holistic education across the sciences, social sciences, arts, humanities, and sports for a multidisciplinary world in order to ensure the unity and integrity of all knowledge.
6. Emphasis on conceptual understanding rather than rote learning and learning-for-exams.
7. Creativity and critical thinking to encourage logical decision-making and innovation.
8. Ethics and human and Constitutional values like empathy, respect for others, cleanliness, courtesy, democratic spirit, spirit of service, respect for public property, scientific temper, liberty, responsibility, pluralism, equality, and justice.
9. Promoting multilingualism and the power of language in teaching and learning.
10. Life skills such as communication, cooperation, teamwork, and resilience.
11. Focus on regular formative assessment for learning rather than the summative assessment that encourages today's coaching culture.
12. Extensive use of technology in teaching and learning, removing language barriers, increasing access for *divyang* students, and educational planning and management.
13. Respect for diversity and respect for the local context in all curriculum, pedagogy, and policy, always keeping in mind that education is a concurrent subject.
14. Full equity and inclusion as the cornerstone of all educational decisions to ensure that all students are able to thrive in the education system.
15. Synergy in curriculum across all levels of education from early childhood care and education to school education to higher education.
16. Teachers and faculty as the heart of the learning process— their recruitment, continuous professional development, positive working environments and service conditions.
17. A 'light but tight' regulatory framework to ensure

integrity, transparency, and resource efficiency of the educational system through audit and public disclosure while encouraging innovation and out-of-the-box ideas through autonomy, good governance, and empowerment.

18. Outstanding research as a corequisite for outstanding education and development.

19. Continuous review of progress based on sustained research and regular assessment by educational experts.

20. A rootedness and pride in India, and its rich, diverse, ancient and modern culture and knowledge systems and traditions.

21. Education is a public service; access to quality education must be considered a basic right of every child.

22. Substantial investment in a strong, vibrant public education system as well as the encouragement and facilitation of true philanthropic private and community participation.

1.3 Vision of NEP, 2020

NEP, 2020 envisions an education system rooted in Indian ethos that contributes directly to transforming India, that is Bharat, sustainably into an equitable and vibrant knowledge society, by providing high-quality education to all, and thereby making India a global knowledge superpower. NEP, 2020 envisages that the curriculum and pedagogy of our institutions must develop among the students a deep sense of respect towards the Fundamental Duties and Constitutional values, bonding with one's country, and a conscious awareness of one's roles and responsibilities in a changing world.

The vision of NEP, 2020 is to instil among the learners a deep-rooted pride in being Indian, not only in thought, but also in spirit, intellect, and deeds, as well as to develop knowledge, skills, values, and dispositions that support responsible commitment to human rights, sustainable development and living, and global well-being, thereby reflecting a truly global citizen.

1.4 School Education

NEP, 2020 envisages that the extant 10+2 structure in school education will be modified with a new pedagogical and curricular restructuring of 5+3+3+4 covering ages 3-18.

Currently, children in the age group of 3-6 are not covered in the 10+2 structure as class 1 begins at age 6. In the new 5+3+3+4 structure, a strong base of Early Childhood Care and Education (ECCE) from age 3 is also included, which is aimed at promoting better overall learning, development, and well-being.

1.4.1 Early Childhood Care and Education: Over 85 percent of a child's cumulative brain development occurs prior to the age of 6, indicating the critical importance of appropriate care and stimulation of the brain in the early years in order to ensure healthy brain development and growth. Presently, quality ECCE is not available to crores of young children, particularly children from socio-economically disadvantaged backgrounds. Strong investment in ECCE has the potential to give all young children such access, enabling them to participate and flourish in the educational system throughout their lives. Universal provisioning of quality early childhood development, care, and education must thus be achieved as soon as possible, and no later than 2030, to ensure that all students entering grade 1 are school ready.

ECCE ideally consists of flexible, multi-faceted, multi-level, play-based, activity-based, and inquiry-based learning, comprising of alphabets, languages, numbers, counting, colours, shapes, indoor and outdoor play, puzzles and logical thinking, problem-solving, drawing, painting and other visual art, craft, drama and puppetry, music and movement. It also includes a focus on developing social capacities, sensitivity, good behaviour, courtesy, ethics, personal and public cleanliness, teamwork, and cooperation. The overall aim of ECCE will be to attain optimal outcomes in the domains of: physical and motor development, cognitive development, socio-emotional-ethical development, cultural and artistic

8   National Education Policy (NEP), 2020 and the Role of Teachers

development, and the development of communication and early language, literacy, and numeracy.

1.4.2 Foundational Literacy and Numeracy: The ability to read and write, and perform basic operations with numbers, is a necessary foundation and an indispensable prerequisite for all future schooling and lifelong learning. However, various governmental, as well as non-governmental surveys, indicate that we are currently in a learning crisis: a large proportion of students currently in elementary school, estimated to be over 5 crore in number, have not attained foundational literacy and numeracy, i.e., the ability to read and comprehend basic text and the ability to carry out basic addition and subtraction with Indian numerals.

Attaining foundational literacy and numeracy for all children will thus become an urgent national mission, with immediate measures to be taken on many fronts and with clear goals that will be attained in the short-term (including that every student attains foundational literacy and numeracy by grade 3). The highest priority of the education system will be to achieve universal foundational literacy and numeracy in primary school by 2025. The rest of NEP, 2020 will become relevant for our students only if this most basic learning requirement (i.e., reading, writing, and arithmetic at the foundational level) is first achieved. To this end, a National Mission on Foundational Literacy and Numeracy will be set up by the Ministry of Education (MoE), Government of India [erstwhile Ministry of Human Resource and Development (MHRD)] on priority. Accordingly, all governments of States and Union Territories will immediately prepare an implementation plan for attaining universal foundational literacy and numeracy in all primary schools, identifying stage-wise targets and goals to be achieved by 2025, and closely tracking and monitoring progress of the same.

1.4.3 Curtailing Dropout Rates: One of the primary goals of the schooling system must be to ensure that children are enrolled in and are attending school. Through initiatives such as the *Sarva Shiksha Abhiyan* (now *Samagra Shiksha*)

Main Provisions of National Education Policy (NEP), 2020   9

and the Right to Education Act, India has made remarkable strides in recent years in attaining near-universal enrolment in elementary education.

There are two overall initiatives that will be undertaken to bring children who have dropped out back to school and to prevent further children from dropping out. The first is to provide effective and sufficient infrastructure so that all students have access to safe and engaging school education at all levels from pre-primary school to grade 12. Besides providing regular trained teachers at each stage, special care shall be taken to ensure that no school remains deficient on infrastructure support. The credibility of Government schools shall be re-established and this will be attained by upgrading and enlarging the schools that already exist, building additional quality schools in areas where they do not exist, and providing safe and practical conveyances and/or hostels, especially for the girl children, so that all children have the opportunity to attend a quality school and learn at the appropriate level. Alternative and innovative education centres will be put in place in cooperation with civil society to ensure that children of migrant labourers, and other children who are dropping out of school due to various circumstances are brought back into mainstream education.

The second is to achieve universal participation in school by carefully tracking students, as well as their learning levels, in order to ensure that they: (a) are enrolled in and attending school, and (b) have suitable opportunities to catch up and re-enter school in case they have fallen behind or dropped out. For providing equitable and quality education from the foundational stage through grade 12 to all children up to the age of 18, suitable facilitating systems shall be put in place. Counsellors or well-trained social workers connected to schools/school complexes and teachers will continuously work with students and their parents and will travel through and engage with communities to ensure that all school-age children are attending and learning in school. Trained and qualified social workers from the civil society organizations/departments of Social Justice and Empowerment and government functionaries dealing with empowerment of persons with disabilities at the State and district level, could be connected to schools, through various innovative mechanisms adopted by State/UT Governments, to help in carrying out this important work.

1.4.4 Curriculum and Pedagogy in Schools: The curricular and pedagogical structure of school education will be reconfigured to make it responsive and relevant to the developmental needs and interests of learners at different stages of their development, corresponding to the age ranges of 3-8, 8-11, 11-14, and 14-18 years, respectively.

The curricular and pedagogical structure and the curricular framework for school education will therefore be guided by a 5+3+3+4 design, consisting of the foundational stage (in two parts, that is, 3 years of *anganwadi*/pre-school + 2 years in primary school in grades 1-2; both together covering ages 3-8), preparatory stage (grades 3-5, covering ages 8-11), middle stage (grades 6-8, covering ages 11-14), and secondary stage (grades 9-12 in two phases, i.e., 9 and 10 in the first and 11 and 12 in the second, covering ages 14-18).

1.4.5 Teachers: To ensure that outstanding students enter the teaching profession, especially from rural areas, a large number of merit-based scholarships shall be instituted across the country for studying quality 4-year integrated B.Ed. programmes. In rural areas, special merit-based scholarships will be established that also include preferential employment in their local areas upon successful completion of their B.Ed. programmes. Such scholarships will provide local job opportunities to local students, especially female students, so that these students serve as local-area role models and as highly qualified teachers who speak the local language. Incentives will be provided for teachers to take up teaching jobs in rural areas, especially in areas that are currently facing acute shortage of quality teachers. A key incentive for teaching in rural schools will be the provision of local housing near or

Main Provisions of National Education Policy (NEP), 2020   11

on the school premises or increased housing allowances.

The harmful practice of excessive teacher transfers will be halted, so that students have continuity in their role models and educational environments. Transfers will occur in very special circumstances, as suitably laid down in a structured manner by State/UT governments. Furthermore, transfers will be conducted through an online computerized system that ensures transparency.

Teacher eligibility tests (TETs) will be strengthened to inculcate better test material, both in terms of content and pedagogy. The TETs will also be extended to cover teachers across all stages (foundational, preparatory, middle and secondary) of school education. For subject teachers, suitable TET test scores in the corresponding subjects will also be taken into account for recruitment. To gauge passion and motivation for teaching, a classroom demonstration or interview will become an integral part of teacher hiring at schools and school complexes. These interviews would also be used to assess comfort and proficiency in teaching in the local language, so that every school/school complex has at least some teachers who can converse with students in the local language and other prevalent home languages of students. Teachers in private schools also must have qualified similarly through TET, a demonstration/interview, and knowledge of local language(s).

To ensure an adequate number of teachers across subjects—particularly in subjects such as arts, physical education, vocational education, and languages—teachers could be recruited to a school or school complex and the sharing of teachers across schools could be considered in accordance with the grouping-of-schools adopted by governments of States and Union Territories.

1.5 Higher Education

Higher education plays an extremely important role in promoting human as well as societal well-being in developing

12 National Education Policy (NEP), 2020 and the Role of Teachers

India as envisioned in its Constitution—a democratic, just, socially conscious, cultured, and humane nation upholding liberty, equality, fraternity, and justice for all. Higher education significantly contributes towards sustainable livelihoods and economic development of the nation. As India moves towards becoming a knowledge economy and society, a greater number of Indians are likely to aspire for higher education.

Given the 21st century requirements, quality higher education must aim to develop good, thoughtful, well-rounded, and creative individuals. It must enable an individual to study one or more specialized areas of interest at a deep level, and also develop character, ethical and Constitutional values, intellectual curiosity, scientific temper, creativity, spirit of service, and 21st century capabilities across a range of disciplines including sciences, social sciences, arts, humanities, languages, as well as professional, technical, and vocational subjects. A quality higher education must enable personal accomplishment and enlightenment, constructive public engagement, and productive contribution to the society. It must prepare students for more meaningful and satisfying lives and work roles and enable economic independence.

For the purpose of developing holistic individuals, it is essential that an identified set of skills and values will be incorporated at each stage of learning, from pre-school to higher education.

At the societal level, higher education must enable the development of an enlightened, socially conscious, knowledgeable, and skilled nation that can find and implement robust solutions to its own problems. Higher education must form the basis for knowledge creation and innovation thereby contributing to a growing national economy. The purpose of quality higher education is, therefore, more than the creation of greater opportunities for individual employment. It represents the key to more vibrant, socially engaged, cooperative communities and a happier, cohesive, cultured, productive, innovative, progressive, and prosperous nation.

1.5.1 Problems: Some of the major problems currently faced by the higher education system in India include the following:

1. A severely fragmented higher educational ecosystem.
2. Less emphasis on the development of cognitive skills and learning outcomes.
3. A rigid separation of disciplines, with early specialisation and streaming of students into narrow areas of study.
4. Limited access particularly in socio-economically disadvantaged areas, with few higher educational institutions (HEIs) that teach in local languages.
5. Limited teacher and institutional autonomy.
6. Inadequate mechanisms for merit-based career management and progression of faculty and institutional leaders.
7. Lesser emphasis on research at most universities and colleges, and lack of competitive peer reviewed research funding across disciplines.
8. Sub-optimal governance and leadership of HEIs.
9. An ineffective regulatory system.
10. Large affiliating universities resulting in low standards of undergraduate education.

1.5.2 Key Changes: NEP, 2020 envisions a complete overhaul and re-energising of the higher education system to overcome these challenges and thereby deliver high-quality higher education, with equity and inclusion. Its vision includes the following key changes to the current system:

1. Moving towards a higher educational system consisting of large, multidisciplinary universities and colleges, with at least one in or near every district, and with more HEIs across India that offer medium of instruction or programmes in local/Indian languages.
2. Moving towards a more multidisciplinary undergraduate education.
3. Moving towards faculty and institutional autonomy.
4. Revamping curriculum, pedagogy, assessment, and student

14 National Education Policy (NEP), 2020 and the Role of Teachers

support for enhanced student experiences.

5. Reaffirming the integrity of faculty and institutional leadership positions through merit appointments and career progression based on teaching, research, and service.
6. Establishment of a National Research Foundation to fund outstanding peer-reviewed research and to actively seed research in universities and colleges.
7. Governance of HEIs by high qualified independent boards having academic and administrative autonomy.
8. Light but tight regulation by a single regulator for higher education.
9. Increased access, equity, and inclusion through a range of measures, including greater opportunities for outstanding public education; scholarships by private/philanthropic universities for disadvantaged and underprivileged students; online education, and open distance learning (ODL); and all infrastructure and learning materials accessible and available to learners with disabilities.

1.5.3 Institutional Restructuring and Consolidation: The main thrust of this policy regarding higher education is to end the fragmentation of higher education by transforming higher education institutions into large multidisciplinary universities, colleges, and HEI clusters/knowledge hubs, each of which will aim to have 3,000 or more students. This would help build vibrant communities of scholars and peers, break down harmful silos, enable students to become well-rounded across disciplines including artistic, creative, and analytic subjects as well as sports, develop active research communities across disciplines including cross-disciplinary research, and increase resource efficiency, both material and human, across higher education.

Moving to large multidisciplinary universities and HEI clusters is thus the highest recommendation of this policy regarding the structure of higher education. The ancient Indian universities Takshashila, Nalanda, Vallabhi, and Vikramshila, which had thousands of students from India and the world studying in vibrant multidisciplinary environments, amply demonstrated the type of great success that large multidisciplinary research and teaching universities could bring. India urgently needs to bring back this great Indian tradition to create well-rounded and innovative individuals, and which is already transforming other countries educationally and economically.

This vision of higher education will require, in particular, a new conceptual perception/understanding for what constitutes a higher education institution (HEI), i.e., a university or a college. A university will mean a multidisciplinary institution of higher learning that offers undergraduate and graduate programmes, with high quality teaching, research, and community engagement. The definition of university will thus allow a spectrum of institutions that range from those that place equal emphasis on teaching and research i.e., research-intensive universities, those that place greater emphasis on teaching but still conduct significant research i.e. teaching-intensive universities.

Meanwhile, an autonomous degree-granting college (AC) will refer to a large multidisciplinary institution of higher learning that grants undergraduate degrees and is primarily focused on undergraduate teaching though it would not be restricted to that and it need not be restricted to that and it would generally be smaller than a typical university.

A stage-wise mechanism for granting graded autonomy to colleges, through a transparent system of graded accreditation, will be established. Colleges will be encouraged, mentored, supported, and incentivized to gradually attain the minimum benchmarks required for each level of accreditation. Over a period of time, it is envisaged that every college would develop into either an autonomous degree-granting college, or a constituent college of a university—in the latter case, it would be fully a part of the university. With appropriate accreditations, autonomous degree-granting colleges could evolve into research-intensive or teaching-intensive universities, if they so aspire.

1.5.4 Holistic and Multidisciplinary Education: India has a long tradition of holistic and multi-disciplinary learning, from universities such as Takshashila and Nalanda, to the extensive literatures of India combining subjects across fields. Ancient Indian literary works such as Banabhatta's Kadambari described a good education as knowledge of the 64 *kalaas* or arts; and among these 64 arts were not only subjects, such as singing and painting, but also scientific fields, such as chemistry and mathematics, vocational fields such as carpentry and clothes-making, professional fields, such as medicine and engineering, as well as soft skills such as communication, discussion, and debate. The very idea that all branches of creative human endeavour, including mathematics, science, vocational subjects, professional subjects, and soft skills should be considered arts, has distinctly Indian origins. This notion of a 'knowledge of many arts' or what in modern times is often called the 'liberal arts' (i.e. a liberal notion of the arts) must be brought back to Indian education, as it is exactly the kind of education that will be required for the 21st century.

1.5.5 Optimal Learning Environment: Effective learning requires a comprehensive approach that involves appropriate curriculum, engaging pedagogy, continuous formative assessment, and adequate student support. The curriculum must be interesting and relevant, and updated regularly to align with the latest knowledge requirements and to meet specified learning outcomes. High-quality pedagogy is then necessary to successfully impart the curricular material to students; pedagogical practices determine the learning experiences that are provided to students, thus directly influencing learning outcomes. The assessment methods must be scientific, designed to continuously improve learning and test the application of knowledge. Last but not least, the development of capacities that promote student wellness such as fitness, good health, psycho-social well-being, and sound ethical grounding are also critical for high-quality learning.

Thus, curriculum, pedagogy, continuous assessment, and

Main Provisions of National Education Policy (NEP), 2020   17

student support are the cornerstones for quality learning. Along with providing suitable resources and infrastructure, such as quality libraries, classrooms, labs, technology, sports/recreation areas, student discussion spaces, and dining areas, a number of initiatives will be required to ensure that learning environments are engaging and supportive, and enable all students to succeed.

1.5.6 Internationalization: India will be promoted as a global study destination providing premium education at affordable costs thereby helping to restore its role as a *vishwa guru*. An international students office at each HEI hosting foreign students will be set up to coordinate all matters relating to welcoming and supporting students arriving from abroad. Research/teaching collaborations and faculty/student exchanges with high-quality foreign institutions will be facilitated, and relevant mutually beneficial memorandums of understanding (MoUs) with foreign countries will be signed. High performing Indian universities will be encouraged to set up campuses in other countries, and similarly, selected universities e.g., those from among the top 100 universities in the world will be facilitated to operate in India. A legislative framework facilitating such entry will be put in place, and such universities will be given special dispensation regarding regulatory, governance, and content norms on par with other autonomous institutions of India.

Furthermore, research collaboration and student exchanges between Indian institutions and global institutions will be promoted through special efforts. Credits acquired in foreign universities will be permitted, where appropriate as per the requirements of each HEI, to be counted for the award of a degree.

1.5.7 Motivated, Energized, and Capable Faculty: The most important factor in the success of higher education institutions is the quality and engagement of its faculty. Acknowledging the criticality of faculty in achieving the goals of higher education, various initiatives have been introduced in the past several years to systematize recruitment and career

18 National Education Policy (NEP), 2020 and the Role of Teachers

progression, and to ensure equitable representation from various groups in the hiring of faculty. Compensation levels of permanent faculty in public institutions have also been increased substantially. Various initiatives have also been taken towards providing faculty with professional development opportunities. However, despite these various improvements in the status of the academic profession, faculty motivation in terms of teaching, research, and service in HEIs remains far lower than the desired level. The various factors that lie behind low faculty motivation levels must be addressed to ensure that each faculty member is happy, enthusiastic, engaged, and motivated towards advancing her/his students, institution, and profession. To this end, the policy recommends the following initiatives to achieve the best, motivated, and capable faculty in HEIs.

As the most basic step, all HEIs will be equipped with the basic infrastructure and facilities, including clean drinking water, clean working toilets, blackboards, offices, teaching supplies, libraries, labs, and pleasant classroom spaces and campuses. Every classroom shall have access to the latest educational technology that enables better learning experiences.

Teaching duties also will not be excessive, and student-teacher ratios not too high, so that the activity of teaching remains pleasant and there is adequate time for interaction with students, conducting research, and other university activities. Faculty will be appointed to individual institutions and generally not be transferable across institutions so that they may feel truly invested in, connected to, and committed to their institution and community.

Faculty will be given the freedom to design their own curricular and pedagogical approaches within the approved framework, including textbook and reading material selections, assignments, and assessments. Empowering the faculty to conduct innovative teaching, research, and service as they see best will be a key motivator and enabler for them to do truly outstanding, creative work.

Excellence will be further incentivized through appropriate rewards, promotions, recognitions, and movement into institutional leadership. Meanwhile, faculty not delivering on basic norms will be held accountable.

In keeping with the vision of autonomous institutions empowered to drive excellence, HEIs will have clearly defined, independent, and transparent processes and criteria for faculty recruitment. Whereas the current recruitment process will be continued, a 'tenure-track' i.e., suitable probation period shall be put in place to further ensure excellence. There shall be a fast-track promotion system for recognizing high impact research and contribution. A system of multiple parameters for proper performance assessment, for the purposes of 'tenure' i.e., confirmed employment after probation, promotion, salary increases, recognitions, etc., including peer and student reviews, innovations in teaching and pedagogy, quality and impact of research, professional development activities, and other forms of service to the institution and the community, shall be developed by each HEI and clearly enunciated in its institutional development plan (IDP).

The presence of outstanding and enthusiastic institutional leaders that cultivate excellence and innovation is the need of the hour. Outstanding and effective institutional leadership is extremely important for the success of an institution and of its faculty. Excellent faculty with high academic and service credentials as well as demonstrated leadership and management skills will be identified early and trained through a ladder of leadership positions. Leadership positions shall not remain vacant, but rather an overlapping time period during transitions in leadership shall be the norm to ensure the smooth running of institutions. Institutional leaders will aim to create a culture of excellence that will motivate and incentivize outstanding and innovative teaching, research, institutional service, and community outreach from faculty members and all HEI leaders.

20 National Education Policy (NEP), 2020 and the Role of Teachers

1.6 Other Key Areas of Focus

1.6.1 Professional Education: Preparation of professionals must involve an education in the ethic and importance of public purpose, an education in the discipline, and an education for practice. It must centrally involve critical and interdisciplinary thinking, discussion, debate, research, and innovation. For this to be achieved, professional education should not take place in the isolation of one's specialty.

Professional education thus becomes an integral part of the overall higher education system. Stand-alone agricultural universities, legal universities, health science universities, technical universities, and stand-alone institutions in other fields, shall aim to become multidisciplinary institutions offering holistic and multidisciplinary education. All institutions offering either professional or general education will aim to organically evolve into institutions/clusters offering both seamlessly and in an integrated manner by 2030.

1.6.2 Adult Education and Lifelong Learning: The opportunity to attain foundational literacy, obtain an education, and pursue a livelihood must be viewed as basic rights of every citizen. Literacy and basic education open up whole new worlds of personal, civic, economic, and lifelong-learning opportunities for individuals that enable them to progress personally and professionally. At the level of society and the nation, literacy and basic education are powerful force multipliers which greatly enhance the success of all other developmental efforts. Worldwide data on nations indicate extremely high correlations between literacy rates and per capita gross domestic product (GDP).

Meanwhile, being a non-literate member of a community, has innumerable disadvantages, including the inability to: carry out basic financial transactions; compare the quality/quantity of goods purchased against the price charged; fill out forms to apply for jobs, loans, services, etc.; comprehend public circulars and articles in the news media; use conventional and electronic mail to communicate and

Main Provisions of National Education Policy (NEP), 2020　21

conduct business; make use of the internet and other technology to improve one's life and profession; comprehend directions and safety directives on the street, on medicines, etc.; help children with their education; be aware of one's basic rights and responsibilities as a citizen of India; appreciate works of literature; and pursue employment in medium or high-productivity sectors that require literacy. The abilities listed here are an illustrative list of outcomes to be achieved through adoption of innovative measures for adult education.

Extensive field studies and analyses, both in India and across the world, clearly demonstrate that volunteerism and community involvement and mobilization are key success factors of adult literacy programmes, in conjunction with political will, organizational structure, proper planning, adequate financial support, and high-quality capacity building of educators and volunteers. Successful literacy programmes result not only in the growth of literacy among adults, but also result in increased demand for education for all children in the community, as well as greater community contribution to positive social change. The National Literacy Mission, when it was launched in 1988, was largely based on the voluntary involvement and support of the people, and resulted in significant increase in national literacy during the period of 1991-2011, including among women, and also initiated dialogue and discussions on pertinent social issues of the day.

Strong and innovative government initiatives for adult education—in particular, to facilitate community involvement and smooth and beneficial integration of technology—will be affected as soon as possible to expedite this all-important aim of achieving 100 percent literacy.

1.6.3 Promotion of Indian Languages, Arts, and Culture: India is a treasure trove of culture, developed over thousands of years and manifested in the form of arts, works of literature, customs, traditions, linguistic expressions, artefacts, heritage sites, and more. Crores of people from around the world partake in, enjoy, and benefit from this cultural wealth daily, in the form of

22 National Education Policy (NEP), 2020 and the Role of Teachers

visiting India for tourism, experiencing Indian hospitality, purchasing India's handicrafts and handmade textiles, reading the classical literature of India, practicing yoga and meditation, being inspired by Indian philosophy, participating in India's unique festivals, appreciating India's diverse music and art, and watching Indian films, amongst many other aspects. It is this cultural and natural wealth that truly makes India, "Incredible India", as per India's tourism slogan. The preservation and promotion of India's cultural wealth must be considered a high priority for the country, as it is truly important for the nation's identity as well as for its economy.

The promotion of Indian arts and culture is important not only for the nation but also for the individual. Cultural awareness and expression are among the major competencies considered important to develop in children, in order to provide them with a sense of identity, belonging, as well as an appreciation of other cultures and identities. It is through the development of a strong sense and knowledge of their own cultural history, arts, languages, and traditions that children can build a positive cultural identity and self-esteem. Thus, cultural awareness and expression are important contributors both to individual as well as societal well-being.

The arts form a major medium for imparting culture. The arts—besides strengthening cultural identity, awareness, and uplifting societies—are well known to enhance cognitive and creative abilities in individuals and increase individual happiness. The happiness/well-being, cognitive development, and cultural identity of individuals are important reasons that Indian arts of all kinds must be offered to students at all levels of education, starting with early childhood care and education.

Language, of course, is inextricably linked to art and culture. Different languages 'see' the world differently, and the structure of a language, therefore, determines a native speaker's perception of experience. In particular, languages influence the way people of a given culture speak with others, including with family members, authority figures, peers, and strangers, and influence the tone of conversation. The tone, perception of experience, and familiarity (*apnapan*) inherent in conversations among speakers of a common language are a reflection and record of a culture. Culture is, thus, encased in our languages. Art, in the form of literature, plays, music, film, etc. cannot be fully appreciated without language. In order to preserve and promote culture, one must preserve and promote a culture's languages.

1.6.4 Technology Use and Integration: India is a global leader in information and communication technology and in other cutting-edge domains, such as space. The Digital India Campaign is helping to transform the entire nation into a digitally empowered society and knowledge economy. While education will play a critical role in this transformation, technology itself will play an important role in the improvement of educational processes and outcomes; thus, the relationship between technology and education at all levels is bidirectional.

Given the explosive pace of technological development allied with the sheer creativity of tech-savvy teachers and entrepreneurs including student entrepreneurs, it is certain that technology will impact education in multiple ways, only some of which can be foreseen at the present time. New technologies involving artificial intelligence, machine learning, block chains, smart boards, handheld computing devices, adaptive computer testing for student development, and other forms of educational software and hardware will not just change what students learn in the classroom but how they learn, and thus these areas and beyond will require extensive research both on the technological as well as educational fronts.

Use and integration of technology to improve multiple aspects of education will be supported and adopted, provided these interventions are rigorously and transparently evaluated in relevant contexts before they are scaled up. An autonomous body, the National Educational Technology Forum (NETF), will be created to provide a platform for the free exchange of ideas on the use of technology to enhance learning, assessment, planning, administration, and so on, both for school and higher education. The aim of the NETF will be to facilitate decision making on the induction, deployment, and use of technology, by providing to the leadership of educational institutions, Central and State governments, and other stakeholders, the latest knowledge and research as well as the opportunity to consult and share best practices.

1.6.5 Online and Digital Education: New circumstances and realities require new initiatives. The recent rise in epidemics and pandemics necessitates that we are ready with alternative modes of quality education whenever and wherever traditional and in-person modes of education are not possible. In this regard, NEP, 2020 recognizes the importance of leveraging the advantages of technology while acknowledging its potential risks and dangers. It calls for carefully designed and appropriately scaled pilot studies to determine how the benefits of online/digital education can be reaped while addressing or mitigating the downsides. In the meantime, the existing digital platforms and ongoing ICT-based educational initiatives must be optimized and expanded to meet the current and future challenges in providing quality education for all.

However, the benefits of online/digital education cannot be leveraged unless the digital divide is eliminated through concerted efforts, such as the Digital India campaign and the availability of affordable computing devices. It is important that the use of technology for online and digital education adequately addresses concerns of equity.

Teachers require suitable training and development to be effective online educators. It cannot be assumed that a good teacher in a traditional classroom will automatically be a good teacher in an online classroom. Aside from changes required in pedagogy, online assessments also require a different approach. There are numerous challenges to conducting online examinations at scale, including limitations on the types of questions that can be asked in an online environment, handling

Main Provisions of National Education Policy (NEP), 2020   25

network and power disruptions, and preventing unethical practices. Certain types of courses/subjects, such as performing arts and science practical have limitations in the online/digital education space, which can be overcome to a partial extent with innovative measures. Further, unless online education is blended with experiential and activity-based learning, it will tend to become a screen-based education with limited focus on the social, affective and psychomotor dimensions of learning.

1.7 Implementation of NEP, 2020

Implementation will be guided by the following principles. First, implementation of the spirit and intent of NEP, 2020 will be the most critical matter. Second, it is important to implement the policy initiatives in a phased manner, as each policy point has several steps, each of which requires the previous step to be implemented successfully. Third, prioritization will be important in ensuring optimal sequencing of policy points, and that the most critical and urgent actions are taken up first, thereby enabling a strong base. Fourth, comprehensiveness in implementation will be key; as NEP, 2020 is interconnected and holistic, only a full-fledged implementation, and not a piecemeal one, will ensure that the desired objectives are achieved. Fifth, since education is a concurrent subject, it will need careful planning, joint monitoring, and collaborative implementation between the Centre and States. Sixth, timely infusion of requisite resources, human, infrastructural, and financial, at the Central and State levels will be crucial for the satisfactory execution of NEP, 2020. Finally, careful analysis and review of the linkages between multiple parallel implementation steps will be necessary in order to ensure effective dovetailing of all initiatives. This will also include early investment in some of the specific actions (such as the setting up of early childhood care and education infrastructure) that will be imperative to ensuring a strong base and a smooth progression for all subsequent programmes and actions.

Subject-wise implementation committees of experts in cooperation and consultation with other relevant Ministries will be set up at both the Central and State levels to develop detailed implementation plans for each aspect of NEP, 2020 in accordance with the above principles to achieve the goals of NEP, 2020 in a clear and phased manner. Yearly joint reviews of the progress of implementation of the policy, in accordance with the targets set for each action, will be conducted by designated teams constituted by MoE and the States, and reviews will be shared with Central Advisory Board of Education (CABE). In the decade of 2030-40, the entire policy will be in an operational mode, following which another comprehensive review will be undertaken.

2

Education and the Role of Teachers

Human life which is the best creation of God has got two parts: the biological and sociological or cultural. While the former is maintained and transmitted by food and imitation, the latter is preserved and transmitted by education. Biological aspect is found in plant and animal life also. However, the sociological or cultural aspect is the rare dissimilarity of human life alone. It is only a human being which is capable of being educated.

2.1 Why Education is Essential?

Since the dawn of Independence in 1947, efforts have been made to raise the standard of living of the masses. The success of such efforts, along with other factors, depends to a great extent on the quality of manpower which, in turn, is influenced by the standard of education in the country. India's future depends on the quantity and quality of education.

Education is essential for everyone. It is the level of education that helps people earn respect and recognition. It is a vital part of life—both personally and socially. However, the unequal standard of education is still a major problem that needs to be solved.

Through education, a person tries to seek new ideas and ways of life. It is again through education that he promotes his intelligence and adds his knowledge with which he can move in the world for good or for the evil, according to his needs. Thus, a person attempts to understand himself/herself in relation to the world around him/her and transmits the knowledge gained to the succeeding generations. His life in this complex world is governed not only by the biological processes, but also by social processes. Education is one of the major *life-processes* in an individual. Just as there are certain indispensable vital processes of life in the biological sense, so also, education may be considered a vital process in a social sense. Education is indispensable for normal living. Without education, an individual would be unqualified for further growing.

2.2 Education and Development

The importance of education for the development of a country must not be underestimated because education is a tool which alone can inculcate national and cultural values and liberate people of false prejudice, ignorance and representations. Education provides the required knowledge, techniques, skills and information and enables people to understand their rights and duties towards their family, society and motherland at large. Education expands the vision and outlook, provokes the spirit of healthy competition and a desire to advance for the achievements of one's consciousness, regenerating truth, and thereby the capability to fight ignorance, injustice, corruption, violence, disparity and communalism—the greatest hazards to the progress of a nation. Although education has a significant influence on life, average education is not the same in all the areas.

As a result, strategies are being made to resolve these problems. Without education, life would be disastrous and detrimental. Consequently, governments around the world are trying their best to make education accessible to everyone, particularly the poor and the disabled. There are still some places where the inhabitants are almost completely uneducated, causing a serious lack of knowledge.

Additionally, every child should be given equal opportunities to learn and study. Since, the development of a country depends vastly on the standard of education, the governments must do everything in their power to improve it. Although the educational system of different countries is not similar, yet they should share a common goal to provide their citizens with a suitable and proper learning.

Education and the Role of Teachers

The pivotal role of education in accelerating the pace of all-round development—specifically in economic, social, technological, and industrial development—has been recognized in successive national plans.

2.3 Teachers as Catalysts of the Society

Teachers are an extremely important aspect of any society for a multitude of reasons. Teachers are people who educate the youth of a society who, in turn, become leaders of the next generation of people. Teachers are people instrumental in imparting knowledge to children when they are in their most impressionable years. Things which children learn from their teachers at a very young age are most likely to stay with them, in one form or the other for the rest of their lives.

Certainly, teachers have a significant mark on the development of young children and even older children alike, as they are teaching them and helping them develop their knowledge so that they can go on in life and be responsible and productive members of the society. According to Henry Adams, "A teacher affects eternity; he can never tell where an influence stops". [1]

According to National Education Policy (NEP), 2020, "the teacher must be at the centre of the fundamental reforms in the education system. The new education policy must help re-establish teachers, at all levels, as the most respected and essential members of our society, because they truly shape our next generation of citizens. It must do everything to empower teachers and help them to do their job as effectively as possible. The New Education Policy must help recruit the very best and brightest to enter the teaching profession at all levels, by ensuring livelihood, respect, dignity, and autonomy, while also instilling in the system, basic methods of quality control and accountability". [2]

Our ancestors have given third spot to a teacher in the society, the first being allotted to the mother, second to the father and fourth to the God. The influence of the first two is inevitable for each and every child in their home environment and simultaneously, a child proceeds to the next sacred place of learning, i.e. the school. Accordingly, it is said, a parent is the first teacher of a child and teacher is the second parent of a child.

As every person has been to school up until at least a certain point in his or her life, one can attest to the fact that an ethical teacher, who truly cares about his/her responsibilities, can definitely have a profound effect on his/her students. A student will become significantly more interested in learning, if his or her teacher is really invested in teaching a particular subject matter. If a teacher finds a way to engage his or her students in an interesting yet informative manner, the students will certainly develop a thirst for learning and acquiring knowledge.

A teacher is one who imparts knowledge to the pupils. When a teacher is doing or helping someone else to learn, he or she is teaching. It is also important to keep in mind that the quality of teaching is directly related to the quality and value of learning.

In a way, all the teachers engaged in teaching profession, from kindergarten to the university level, may not be teaching or behaving uniformly well to the satisfaction of their students, at least in the classroom. We expect that a teacher should be a good role model or a leader so as to be imitated by his/her students both within and outside the classroom situations. The inter-relationship between the teachers and the taught is well expressed with a degree of difference among teachers through a good saying viz., "a mediocre teacher tells; a good teacher explains; superior teachers demonstrate; and great teachers inspire". [3]

In the above classification, the last category would be highly limited and perhaps a majority of them would come in the first category and the rest may come under the remaining two categories. Schools are nurseries of a nation and the teachers are architects of the future society. Therefore, the role

Education and the Role of Teachers 31

of teachers is crucial in the teaching-learning process. Though words like teacher effectiveness, teacher competence or teaching success are used synonymously, the connotations are different. A great teacher is one whom a student remembers and cherishes forever. Teachers have a long-lasting impact on the lives of their students, and a great teacher inspires students towards greatness.

The present day teachers in India are a by-product of the emergence of middle class in the latter half of the 19th century. But for the striking similarities between the jobs which the past and present teachers have performed, or continue to perform, the differences and distinctions in their social and economic position are so pronounced that one could ignore them only at the risk of perpetuating a myth—a legend which is as misleading as it is false.

2.4 Qualities of a Good Teacher

A perfect teacher has to be up-to-date and future-oriented. He/she is charged with the responsibility of building up a nation through better teaching, good human relationships and problem-solving attitude. Incidentally, this problem-solving approach has been an important change in ever increasing complexities thrust upon teachers to augment their skills in resolving problems.

In reality, every commission which has examined the educational problems of the country has drawn specific attention towards the teachers. The Secondary Education Commission (1952-53) opined, "we are, however, convinced that the most important factor in the contemplated educational reconstruction is the teacher—his personal qualities, his educational qualifications, his professional training and the place which he occupies in the school as well as in the community.

The reputation of a school and its influence on the life of the community invariably depends on the kind of teachers working in it. Priority of consideration must, therefore, be

32 National Education Policy (NEP), 2020 and the Role of Teachers

given to the various problems concerned with the improvement of their status". [4]

Talented teachers are able to work with students with varying levels of maturity and knowledge. Teachers often serve as mentors for their students. The desire to influence students positively is a core motivation for many teachers when they enter into the profession. In no profession, maturity is more important, than in teaching. Students experience emotional ups and downs, and insightful teachers are able to sense the changes and respond to them appropriately. Teachers must be pillars, consistently encouraging students to grow as human beings and advance academically.

Maintaining good community relations is an inherent part of being a teacher, and contact with parents, administrators, and community leaders enhances their effectiveness in the classroom. Teaching encompasses far more than passing information from teachers to students. Teachers should be illuminators who can provide their students not only with interesting and useful material, but also with a vision of where they might end up if they learn well.

Perhaps, the most important thing teachers communicate to students and to the community is a sense of satisfaction, with their choice of teaching as their life mission. Teaching at its highest level is a calling, and good teachers feel it to their core.

Excellent teachers never lose enthusiasm of their profession. They might become temporarily burdened by the administrative hassles or any isolated problem, but their underlying engagement with the profession is unwavering. Students feel this energy, and teachers who project it are much more successful than those who do it.

Education is one of the greatest services provided by the teachers. The role played by teachers is a very vital component in the course of nation building. Teachers work in close co-ordination with students to help them in building up their future. They facilitate the students in honing their skills or

Education and the Role of Teachers 33

improvise them, impart good habits/attitudes and help them become good citizens. Students tend to follow their teachers in almost every way including manners, style etc. and are influenced by the teacher's affection as well as love for them. Invariably, a teacher should have professional competence as well as good moral background in order to impart these values to students.

Advancement in knowledge dissemination following the success in teaching modules has increased the knowledge base. Everything starts with teachers and the mentality they possess, drives students to newer levels.

2.5 Teacher-Student Relationship

There is a positive correlation between a teacher's professional concentration and students' modelling, featuring him/her. A positive correlation has been observed between a teacher's attachment to the subject and that of the students. The fact that teachers have positive expectations from the students, affects their behaviour. In short, the attributes of a teacher's behaviour is an important variable for the educational system to achieve its objectives.

Teaching is a term which represents a position in educational organizations coupled with a set of behavioural aspects, necessitated by this very position and expresses the status, duties, and relationships of that position. Teaching is an inspiring art. It is impossible to detach a teacher and teaching. The teacher, in fact, mirrors himself in a child and puts an indelible stamp on a young and growing mind.

Whenever a study about teacher and teaching in the context of organizational behaviour is conducted, the functional aspects of an employee within the educational organization are analyzed.

An analysis of the variables determining the behaviour of a teacher in a class-setting in terms of organizational behaviour obviously reveals that one of the major factors determining a teacher's behaviour is the attitude of teacher towards the

34 National Education Policy (NEP), 2020 and the Role of Teachers

teaching profession.

The role of a teacher in an educational process is always challenging and vibrant. A teacher's work is not only limited to the spread of knowledge but much more than that. One of the primal tasks of a teacher is to inspire and motivate students towards the exquisite goals. The teacher in a naturalistic set up is only a setter of the stage, a supplier of material and opportunities, a provider of an ideal environment, and a creator of conditions under which the natural development takes place. Teaching is a core profession and one of the key agents of change in today's knowledge society. Teacher quality, training and continuous professional development is not only vital for the improvement of our education system but also for achieving the earmarked goals of education.

In conclusion, education is absolutely beneficial for the society as a whole. A robust and an evolving education system is need of the hour to eradicate illiteracy and also to provide common man with an access not only to basic education but also higher and technical education.

Teacher is one of the important ingredients of an education system. The standard of education in India, as in any other country, depends on the quality and positive attitude of teachers. Whatever means are adopted for improving the education system nothing can be achieved if the teachers concerned do not possess the requisite intellectual and professional abilities. It would be wise to quote, that a teacher is the heart an educational institution and success of the institution in attaining its goals, would largely depend on the quality of its teachers.

Endnotes

1. Henry, Adams (1999), "The Education of Henry Adams", Oxford University Press.
2. Government of India, Ministry of Human Resource Development, "National Education Policy, 2020", p. 4.
3. Gerald, Anderson (2009), "Achieving Teaching Excellence: A Step-by-Step Guide", A1 Book Co.

4. "Report of the Secondary Education Commission. (1952-53)", Ministry of Education, New Delhi.

3

Education and Socio-economic Development

Human beings are the heartbeat of a country. Intangible assets, like human capital, decide the use of tangible and material resources to fulfil the objectives of any society. Since people constitute the most significant resource of any country, human development becomes critical for its socio-economic progress. Human resources in terms of demographic trends are important, as also the development of human resources through programmes in education, health, social welfare and science and technology.

3.1 Human Resources and Development

Human resources are of critical importance for the growth of knowledge and technology, value addition and improvement of competitiveness in manufacturing through processes of continuous improvement. In fact, the human resources are the only *appreciating resources* in a manufacturing system. They are the only resources that have the motivation and ability to increase their value if suitable conditions are provided, whereas all other resources—machines, building, materials and so on—depreciate in value with time. The best enterprises view their people as their prime asset and the source of their competitive advantage. Nations that have achieved sustainable competitiveness in manufacturing even when they do not have required raw materials, such as Japan and South Korea, have created systems for the continuous improvement of the capabilities of their human resources.

The notion of human well-being itself is more broadly conceived to include not only consumption of goods and services in general but more specifically to ensure that the basic material requirements of all sections of the population, especially those below the poverty line, are met and that they have access to basic social services such as health and education. Specific focus on these dimensions of social development is necessary because experience shows that economic prosperity, measured in terms of per capita income alone, does not always ensure enrichment in quality of life, as reflected, for instance, in the social indicators on health, longevity, literacy and environmental sustainability.

The ultimate objective of all economic efforts is human development which encompasses quality of life, the level of well-being and access to basic social services. The Fundamental Rights that India's Constitution guarantees to every citizen include the right to life and the right to livelihood is inherent in the right to life. In India, the emphasis on the achievement of higher economic growth along with social justice is manifest in the renewed focus on development initiatives in the social sectors.

Human development insists that everyone should enjoy a minimum level of security. In fact, a system should be built in which the State bears the responsibility for providing and ensuring an elementary or basic level of security, and leaves room for partly or wholly contributory schemes. This will mean that the responsibility to provide a floor will be primarily that of the State, and it will be left to individual citizens to acquire higher levels of security through assumption of responsibility and contributory participation.

Development is the key to progress. It is measured in terms of improvement in the lives of the people and strengthening of the individual's and thereby a nation's capacity to deal with the rest of the world. Development is, therefore, interlinked with the entire social, political and cultural fabric of society. It aims at bringing about qualitative changes leading to an upward movement of the entire social system.

3.2 Objectives of Education
Human resources development has necessarily to be

38 National Education Policy (NEP), 2020 and the Role of Teachers

assigned a key role in any development strategy, particularly in a country with a large population. Trained and educated on sound lines, a large population can itself become an asset in accelerating economic growth and in ensuring social change in desired directions.

Education is of basic importance in the development of a nation. The educational machinery should be geared for the specific tasks which the nation sets itself through so as to make available in the various fields personnel of suitable quality at the required rate. The educational system has also an intimate bearing on the attainment of the general objectives inasmuch as it largely determines the quality of the manpower and the social climate of the community.

In a democratic set up, the role of education becomes crucial, since it can function effectively only if there is an intelligent participation of the masses in the affairs of the country. The success of democracy depends also on the growth of the spirit of co-operation and the sense of disciplined citizenship among the people and on the degree to which it becomes possible to evoke public enthusiasm and build up local leadership.

It is essential that the educational programme helps to train the people to place responsibilities before rights and to keep the self-regarding outlook and the force of the acquisitive instinct within legitimate bounds. The educational system should also satisfy cultural needs, which is essential for the healthy growth of a nation. The system should stimulate the growth of the creative faculties, increase the capacity for enjoyment and develop a spirit of critical appreciation of arts, literature and other creative activities. The fulfilment of the objectives mentioned above, will lead to the development of an integrated personality in the individual, which should be the first and foremost aim of any system of education.

3.3 Education and Social Development

A suitably oriented system of education can facilitate and

Education and Socio-economic Development 39

promote social change and contribute to economic growth, not only by training skilled manpower for specific tasks of development but, what is perhaps even more important, by creating the requisite attitudes and climate. Facilities for universal elementary education are a pre-requisite for equality of opportunity.

Education, broadly perceived as a seamless continuum of life long learning, is essential for human resource development at every age level. In a pack-ay of developmental inputs available to the community, education should form an effective means to improve the status and character of living patterns of the people, help intellectual, social and emotional development of the individuals and to enable them to meet their basic needs of daily life. The long range goal of educational planning is then to make available diverse networks of facilities and programmes for education, combining formal and non-formal modes of learning. It should enable all citizens to acquire literacy, numeracy, computational skills, basic understanding of the surrounding world and functional skills of relevance to daily life and to local environment.

Education is important in the development process for two reasons. First, because education can be viewed as an end in itself as it improves the perception and quality of life of people. Secondly, education leads to formation of human capital and is an important investment for the development process.

Education develops basic skills and abilities and fosters a value system conducive to, and in support of, national development goals, both long-term and immediate. In a world where knowledge is increasing at an exponential rate, the task of education in the diffusion of new knowledge and, at the same time, in the preservation and promotion of what is basic to India's culture and ethos, is both complex and challenging.

3.4 Education and Economic Development

The system of education has a determining influence on

40 National Education Policy (NEP), 2020 and the Role of Teachers

the rate at which economic progress is achieved and the benefits which can be derived from it. Economic development naturally makes growing demands on human resources and in a democratic set-up it calls for values and attitudes in the building up of which the quality of education is an important element.

Education is the most important single factor in achieving rapid economic development and technological progress and in creating a social order founded on the values of freedom, social justice and equal opportunity. Programmes of education lie at the base of the effort to forge the bonds of common citizenship, to harness the energies of the people, and to develop the natural and human resources of every part of the country. Developments in recent years have created a momentum for economic growth; yet, there are large deficiencies in the sphere of education, which must be removed speedily if progress is to be sustained and enduring.

Secondary and higher secondary education are important terminal stages in the system of general education and provide a first stage for linking education with the world of work. It is at this point that options are exercised by the youth to enter the world of employment or to go for technical training or to pursue higher education. With the expansion of the base of education at the elementary stage, increasing number of students, including a large number of first generation learners, would reach secondary education. Facilities have to be provided for their education since such education is the only means of social mobility and economic independence, particularly among the socially disadvantaged. Care has to be taken to ensure that secondary education also prepares them for a long-term career as part of the stock of national man power. Keeping these in view, facilities for secondary education would have to be extended to rural and backward areas and access provided to the weaker and more backward sections of the people, particularly the first generation learners.

Expansion and utilisation of employment opportunities and

Education and Socio-economic Development 41

increase in productivity are strongly influenced by education. In the process of development, education is, therefore, an investment. This investment has to be made well in time to derive full benefits from the overall developmental effort.

3.5 Manpower Planning

One of the important links between education and development is provided by manpower development through vocationalisation of secondary education related to employment. This has to be carefully designed, based on detailed surveys of existing and potential work opportunities and of available educational and training facilities. It should also keep in view the specific roles and responsibilities of the different agencies and ensure coordination at the operational level between the developmental programmes and the educational system. Such a differentiation would normally commence after the secondary stage and may cover varying periods depending upon the vocational area, groups of occupations and the nature and level of skills needed. It envisages deepening of practical bias in the school education to be supplemented by appropriate apprenticeship in actual field, farm or factory situations. It is not necessary to follow a rigid sequence in the order of acquiring the several skills and it should be possible to supplement exclusive vocational training courses with necessary educational component. In a way, suitable linkages need to be established within a system for occupational mobility and career development over one's employment/working life.

3.6 Public-Private-Partnership in Education

India has a long tradition of partnership between the public and private sectors in education. There are four types of schools:
1. Government schools established by state governments as well as some centrally established institutions.
2. Local body schools established by elected local

government bodies.

3. Aided schools, i.e. private schools which receive grants from the government.

4. Private unaided schools.

Most of the growth of secondary schools in the private sector in recent years has occurred among unaided schools. It is essential, therefore, that the private sector's capabilities and potential are tapped through innovative public-private-partnerships, while concurrently stepping up public investment by the Central and State Governments at the secondary level. And given that the presence of private schools varies considerably across States, context-specific solutions need to be promoted.

While private provision in secondary education should be fostered wherever feasible, the government will have to take the prime responsibility to provide access to disadvantaged sections and to bridge the rural/urban, regional, gender and social group gaps. Simultaneously, government must invest in teacher education and accountability, curriculum reform, quality assurance, examinations reform, national assessment capabilities and management information systems, which will require time and significant institutional capacity building to succeed at a national scale.

To sum up, education is the most important lever for social, economic and political transformation. A well-educated population, equipped with the relevant knowledge, attitudes and skills is essential for economic and social development in the 21st century. Education is the most potent tool for socio-economic mobility and a key instrument for building an equitable and just society. Education provides skills and competencies for economic well-being. Education strengthens democracy by imparting to citizens the tools needed to fully participate in the governance process. Education also acts as an integrative force in society, imparting values that foster social cohesion and national identity.

4

Studies Related to Attitude of Teachers towards Teaching: A Review

4.1 Studies Conducted in India

Jain, B. (1982) [1], conducted, "A Study of Classroom Behaviour Patterns of Teachers in Relation to their Attitude towards Profession, Morale and Values".

Findings of the Study:

1. Male teachers devoted more time in asking questions than the female teachers.
2. Teachers with a positive attitude towards child-cantered practices, educational process, and pupils devoted more time in asking questions in the classroom.
3. Young teachers had a more favourable attitude towards teaching, and there was a significant negative relationship between the teaching experience and the teacher attitude towards classroom teaching.
4. Analysis of attitude scores for each of the seven groups involved in the experiment by the difference method as well as by the sign test method for paired observations indicated that for five groups, the change was significant while for two groups, i.e. the control group and audiotape feedback group, it was not.
5. Analysis of teaching competence scores and attitude scores indicated that greater teaching competence and more favourable attitude towards teaching in most cases was associated with the supervisor's presence in the groups.

Patil, G.G. (1984) [2] conducted, "A Differential Study of Intelligence, Interest and Attitude of the B.Ed College Students as Contributory Factors towards Their Achievements in the Compulsory subjects".

44 National Education Policy (NEP), 2020 and the Role of Teachers

Findings of the Study:

1. There was no significant difference between the achievements of male (graduates and post-graduates), and inexperienced and experienced pupil-teachers in four compulsory subjects.

2. There was a significant difference between the scores of males and females and inexperienced and experienced pupil-teachers in respect of intelligence. No significant difference in intelligence was found between graduate and post-graduate teachers.

3. Males and experienced pupil-teachers appeared more intelligent than females and pupil-teachers. In the case of interest, there was a significant difference between males and females and inexperienced and experienced pupil-teachers. Female and experienced pupil-teachers were more interested in teaching than male and inexperienced pupil-teachers. However, no significant difference between graduate and post-graduate pupil-teachers was observed.

4. There was a significant difference between the scores of male and female, inexperienced and experienced pupil-teachers regarding attitude. Female pupil-teachers had a more favourable attitude than pupil-teachers; experience played a great role in the development of a favourable attitude towards the teaching profession. However, no significant difference was visible between graduate and post-graduate pupil-teachers regarding attitude towards the teaching profession.

5. The correlation between intelligence and achievement was higher than the correlation between interest and achievement and also between attitude and achievement.

Rao, R.B. (1986) [3] studied, "The Inter-relationship of Values, Adjustment and Teaching Attitude of Pupil-teachers at Various Levels of Socio-economic Status".

Findings of the Study:

1. The factors that emerged out of analysis of five adjustment, six attitude and ten value variables in order of

Studies Related to Attitude of Teachers towards Teaching 45

merit were adjustment, attitude, citizenship, aesthetic, health and hedonistic.

2. Co-relational inferences indicated that adequate EDAD tended to help very significantly in adjustment in other areas. Its inadequacy impaired sound attitude and knowledge value significantly.

3. In total and upper-lower SES groups, the MPT's had a significantly favourable attitude towards the teaching profession. In all SES groups, the mean-differences were not significant.

4. No Significant sex differences were observed in attitude towards classroom teaching (ATCT). The upper SES group had significantly more favourable attitude than the lower middle SES group in this context.

Sulthana, Parveen (2008) [4] conducted a study on "Attitudes and Adjustment of Prospective Teachers, towards their Professional Training".

Findings of the Study:

1. Prospective teachers were found to have the most favourable attitude.

2. It is noteworthy to find that half of the sample of prospective teachers were having more favourable attitude towards teacher training, internship, curriculum and project works and none were found to be having less favourable and least favourable attitude towards their professional training.

3. It was found that among various parameters included under attitude towards professional training, the highest percentage of mean denoted that the attitude towards the teaching profession was comparatively more favourable than the other areas. It was followed by attitude towards project work, then attitude towards teaching practices, followed by attitude towards teaching practices, and finally, attitude towards co-curricular activities. Least favourable attitude was observed towards the evaluation aspect and curricular activities. The most noteworthy

feature was that the prospective teachers had more favourable attitudes in all the six areas without any exception.

4. Attitudes of prospective teachers did not vary significantly with regards to gender, subject background, socio-economic background and area to which they belong.

Sahaya, R. Mary and Samuel, Manorama (2011) [5] studied, "Relationship between Attitude of the B.Ed Student-Teachers towards Teaching and Academic Achievements".

Findings of the Study:

1. There was a significant difference between the female students-teachers and their male counterparts. The findings of the study noted that there was a significant difference between female student-teachers and male student-teachers while comparing performances in theory and practical curriculum.

2. No significant difference was observed between student-teachers coming from the first generation learners or second generation learners. However, with regards to the dimension of values, the student-teachers hailing from the first generation learners depicted a more favourable attitude towards teaching that the student-teachers hailing from the second generation learners.

3. According to the college entry and overall academic achievement of the students-teachers, the results of the study exhibited that there was a significant difference between student-teachers hailing from second generation compared to first generation.

4. There was also a significant relationship between the overall attitude towards teaching and academic achievements of the student-teachers.

Dwivedi, S. (2012) [6] conducted a research on "Impact of Pre-service Teacher Education on Teaching Competence, Teaching Aptitude and Attitude towards Teaching".

Findings of the Study:

1. There was no significant difference between the attitude

towards teaching of male and female prospective teachers, which means that both the groups of pupil-teachers possessed more or less the same level of attitude towards teaching.

2. Attitude towards teaching does not vary significantly with socio-economic status, meaning that pupils-teachers belonging to any socio-economic status possessed more or less the same attitude towards teaching.

3. Type of institution did not significantly affect the attitude towards teaching of prospective teachers.

4. Gender and socio-economic status did not have any significant impact with respect to attitude towards teaching.

5. Significant interaction between gender and type of institution did not exist with respect to attitude towards teaching, indicating that gender of prospective teachers and the type of institution did not play much role in enhancing the attitude towards teaching.

6. The type of institution and the socio-economic status of a prospective teacher did not impact the attitude towards teaching.

7. Any visible interaction among gender, type of institution and socio-economic status did not exist with respect to attitude towards teaching, which means gender and socio-economic status of the prospective teacher or type of institution mutually did not impact attitude towards teaching.

Parvez, Mohammad and Shakir, Mohd. (2013) [7] studied, "The Attitudes of Prospective Teachers towards Teaching Profession".

Findings of the Study:

1. There was a significant difference in the attitude of prospective teachers studying in private and public B.Ed. institutions towards the teaching profession. Pertinently, the type of institution, either public or private, influenced the attitude of prospective teachers

towards the teaching profession.

2. No significant difference was observed in the attitude of female and male prospective teachers towards the teaching profession. Simply putting, the attitude of female and male prospective teachers was not affected or determined by the respective gender.

3. There was also no significant difference in the attitude of Muslim and non-Muslim prospective teachers towards the teaching profession. In short, the attitude of Muslim and non-Muslim prospective teachers was not affected or determined by their religion.

4. There was also no significant difference observed in the attitude of science and social science prospective teachers towards the teaching profession. In other words, the attitude of science and social science prospective teachers was not affected or determined by their choice of streams.

4.2 Studies Conducted Abroad

Karp, Karen and Silliman (1991) [8] conducted a study on, "Elementary School Teachers' Attitudes towards Mathematics: Impact on Student's Autonomous Learning Skills".

Finding of the Study: Teaching behaviour and instructional methods of elementary school teachers were investigated to determine if teachers with a positive attitude toward mathematics, employed different methods in instructions than those with a negative attitude. Overall, teachers with negative attitudes employed methods that fostered dependency whereas teachers with positive attitudes encouraged student's initiative and independence.

Anderson, Dewayne (1995) [9] studied, "Pre-service Teachers' Attitude towards Children".

Finding of the Study: Pre-service teachers revealed large differences in attitude towards children, associated with age, gender, and major. The most positive were the females in elementary, and the least positive were the males in secondary. Those in special education were the most positive, and those in music, art and physical education were the least positive. Whether these attitudes manifest themselves in the classroom remains unknown.

Monahan, Robert and Others (1996) [10] conducted a study on, "Rural Teacher Attitudes towards Inclusion".

Finding of the Study: Over 60 percent of the respondents indicated that inclusion will not succeed because of resistance from the regular teachers. They do not have the instructional skills and educational background to teach special needs students. Regular teachers preferred sending special needs students to special education classrooms rather than delivering their services in a regular classroom.

Special and regular teachers should demonstrate collaboration with all special needs students in regular classroom sessions. It is important to note that special needs students enhance their social skills while attending a regular classroom and need greater attention and assistance which the regular teachers cannot provide.

Hussain, Shaukat, (2004) [11] conducted a study on, "Effectiveness of Teacher Training in Developing Professional Attitude of Prospective Secondary School Teachers".

Findings of the Study:

1. A majority of teacher training institutions were not successful in developing a positive professional attitude among the prospective teachers.
2. Sex had no effect on the overall development of attitude. However, among females, when compared to males, the difference between the new and the mid-group was less than that of the new and final groups.
3. Female prospective teachers acquired greater mean score compared to the male prospective teachers.
4. No difference was found in the mean score of students studying in co-education and general institutions.
5. Trend of attitude development among male and female prospective teachers was different but the volume of the change was the same.

Marete, Elizabeth C. (2004) [12] deliberated upon, "A Study of Teachers' Attitudes towards the Implementation of Free Primary Education in Public Primary Schools in Kikuyu Division".

Findings of the Study: Major findings of the study led to the conclusion that age, and academic and professional qualifications were not significant determinants of teachers' attitude towards the implementation of FPE whereas gender and teaching experience did influence the teachers attitude. It was recommended that the government should employ more teachers to achieve a teacher-pupil ratio of 1:40. Parents should also be further enlightened regards their role as far as FPE is concerned. Free nursery schools should also be put in place and that the government should increase budget allocation for FPE.

Theurer, J. (2006) [13] conducted a study on, "Tell Me what you know: Pre-service Teachers' Attitudes towards Teaching Comprehension".

Findings of the Study:

1. It was found that a majority of pre-service teachers aligned themselves with valuing comprehension, but when juxtaposed against skills, the pre-service teachers were more divided in their responses. Although the pre-service teachers value comprehension, the value that many of them placed on skills while separated from comprehension suggests that they do not have a strong foundation between skills and strategies and the relationship each has with reading comprehension.

2. Literacy modelled at home was a strong theme for many of the pre-service teachers. None of the forty pre-service teachers in the study recalled comprehension instruction as part of their memories in school. References to comprehension focused on authentic reading engagements at home, reading with siblings or parents, or talking about texts with parents.

Gregory, J.P. and Russell, W.R. (2008) [14] studied,

"Teacher Effectiveness in First Grade: The Importance of Background Qualifications, Attitudes and Instructional Practices for Student Learning".

Finding of the Study: The results indicate that compared to instructional practices, background qualifications have less robust associations with the achievement gains. These findings suggest that the No Child Left Behind Act's "highly qualified teacher" provision, which screens teachers on the basis of their background qualifications, is insufficient in ensuring that classrooms are led by teachers who are effective in enhancing student achievement.

To meet the objective, educational policy needs to be directed towards improving aspects of teaching, including instructional practices and teacher attitudes.

Nuri Baloglu, Engin Karadag (2008) [15] conducted a study on, "Relationship between the Prospective Teacher's Attitudes towards the Teaching profession and their Preferred Coping Strategies with Stress".

Findings of the Study: There was a noticeable statistical meaningful relationship between student-teacher's attitudes toward the teaching profession and some of their preferred coping strategies regarding stress.

Hussain (2011) [16] studied, "Relationship between the Professional Attitudes of Secondary School Teachers with their Teaching Behaviour".

Findings of the Study:
1. A majority of the secondary school teachers did not possess a positive attitude towards the profession.
2. Female secondary school teachers had a more positive attitude towards the profession compared to male secondary school teachers.
3. Teachers working in the public sector institutions were found more committed and satisfied compared to the teachers working in the private sector.
4. Majority of teachers working in the rural areas were more committed and satisfied compared to teachers working in

the urban areas.

Sweeting, Kylie (2011) [17] conducted an explanatory case study on, "Early Years Teachers' Attitudes towards Mathematics". The purpose of the study was to investigate the attitude of practicing early years teachers towards mathematics and establish how these attitudes were formed.

The study revealed that amongst the 20 practicing early years teachers surveyed, 75 percent scored within the positive or strongly positive range with no negative or strongly negative attitudes recorded.

A distinct difference was identified between the strongly positive teachers' and the neutral teachers' scores for the sub-scales of enjoyment and self-confidence. High enjoyment along with high self-confidence was common among the positive teachers, whereas lack of enjoyment and low self-confidence was common with the neutral teachers.

In contrast, no distinct difference was identified between the positive and neutral teachers in the sub-scale of motivation, as a mix of positive and neutral teachers scored above 72 percent whilst two neutral teachers scored below 48 percent. All teachers scored similarly for the sub-scale of value.

4.3 Reflections on Various Studies

A host of researchers have tried to examine various types and areas of relationship between a number of variables including teaching competence, teaching aptitude, attitude towards teaching, pre-service and in-service training etc. Some studies were done with one variable or others related to different variables but hardly any study has been done underlining 'attitude towards teaching' with special reference to sex, locale, stream and educational qualifications as variables.

The perusal of the above mentioned literature related to attitudes of prospective teachers towards teaching profession suggests that a lot of research has been conducted to investigate the attitudes of prospective teachers towards the teaching profession.

However, no specific research has been conducted to study the attitudes of prospective teachers towards teaching profession in which independent variables like sex, locality, choice of stream and educational qualification have been included.

It is also evident from the perusal of the related literature regarding the teaching attitude that attitude does affect quality of a trainee which further gives an idea to the investigator that many other factors also exist which affect teaching attitude and deserve to be noticed by the researchers for further studies. Obviously, teacher attitude of prospective teachers with special reference to their sex, locale, stream and educational qualification being important variables make a composite area for research.

Endnotes

1. Jain, B. (1982), "A Study of Classroom Behaviour Patterns of Teachers in Relation to their Attitude towards Profession, Morale and Values", D.Phil. (Edu.) JMI, Third Survey of Research in Education, 1978-1983, 763.

2. Patil, G.G. (1984), "A Differential Study of Intelligence, Interest and Attitude of the B.Ed. College Students as Contributory Factors towards their Achievements in the Compulsory Subjects", Buch, M.B., Fourth Survey (1983-1988) of Research in Education, 971.

3. Rao, R.B. (1986), "A Study of Inter-relationship of Values, Adjustment and Teaching-Attitude of Pupil-Teachers at Various Levels of Socio-economic Status", Buch, M.B., Fourth Survey (1983-1988) of Research in Education, Baroda Society for Educational Research and Development, II, 980.

4. Parveen, Sulthana (2008), "Attitudes and Adjustments of Prospective Teachers towards their Professional Training", M.Phil. Dissertation, Acharya Nagarjuna University.

5. Sahaya, Mary R. and Manorama Samuel (2011), "Relationship between Attitude of the B.Ed. Student-Teachers towards Teaching and Academic Achievement", Edutracks, Neelkamal, Hyderabad, February, 10(6), 28-35.

6. Dwivedi, Shri Kant (2012), "Impact of Pri-service Teacher

Education on Teaching Competence, Teaching Aptitude and Attitude towards Teaching", Ph.D. thesis, IASE, MJP Rohilkhand University, Bareilly.

7. Parvez, Mohammad and Mohd. Shakir (2013), "Attitudes of Prospective Teachers towards Teaching Profession", *Journal of Education and Practice*, 4, (10).

8. Karp-Karen-Silliman (1991), "Elementary School Teachers Attitudes towards Mathematics: The Impact of Student's Autonomous Learning Skills".

9. Anderson-DeWayne, B., Anderson Ariel, L.H. (1995), "Pre-service Teachers' Attitudes towards Children: Implications for Teacher Education", *Educational Forum*, 59(3), 312-318.

10. Monahan, Robert G. and Others (1996), "Rural Teacher Attitudes towards Inclusion".

11. Hussain, Shaukat (2004), **"Effectiveness of Teacher Training in Developing Professional Attitude of Prospective Secondary School Teachers"**, Ph.D. thesis, University of Arid Agriculture, Rawalpindi, available at: eprints.hec.gov.pk.

12. Marete, Elizabeth Cirindi (2004), "A Study of Teachers' Attitudes towards the Implementation of Free Primary Education in Public Primary Schools in Kikuyu Division".

13. Theurer, J. (2006), "Tell me what you know; Pare-service Teachers' Attitudes towards Teaching Comprehension", *The Reading Matrix*, 6, 113-120.

14. Gregory, J.P. and Russell, W.R. (2008), **"Teacher Effectiveness in First Grade: The Importance of Background Qualifications, Attitudes and Instructional Practices for Student Learning"**, *Journal of Educational Evaluation and Policy Analysis*, 30, (2), 111-140, Sage Publications.

15. Nuri, Baloglu and Engin Karadag (2008), "A Study of the Relationship between the Prospective Teachers Attitudes towards the Teaching Profession and their Preferred Coping Strategies with Stress", available at: http://www.educationalrev.us.edu.pl/e19/a21.pdf.

16. Hussain et al. (2011), "Relationship between the Professional Attitudes of Secondary School Teachers with their Teaching Behaviour", *International Journal of Academic Research in Business and Social Sciences*, 3, 38-46.

17. Sweeting, Kylie (2011), "Early Years Teachers' Attitudes towards Mathematics", M.Ed. dissertation, Centre for Learning Innovation, Faculty of Education, Queensland University of Technology.

5

Attitude of Teachers towards Teaching

"Teachers truly shape the future of our children and, therefore, the future of our nation. It is because of this noblest role that the teacher in India was the most respected member of society. Only the very best and most learned became teachers. Society gave teachers, or gurus, what they needed to pass on their knowledge, skills, and ethics optimally to students. The quality of teacher education, recruitment, deployment, service conditions, and empowerment of teachers is not where it should be, and consequently the quality and motivation of teachers does not reach the desired standards. The high respect for teachers and the high status of the teaching profession must be restored so as to inspire the best to enter the teaching profession. The motivation and empowerment of teachers is required to ensure the best possible future for our children and our nation".

—National Education Policy, 2020, p. 20.

Teaching being an interactive process, it has been realized that a teacher's behaviour in the classroom is chiefly responsible for the proper educational growth of pupils. The effectiveness of the process of education has been squarely acknowledged to depend upon the teaching attitude of teachers. It may not be considered in anyways as an exaggerated statement, that it is the teaching attitude of the teachers which is primal in any system of education. This leads one to enunciate that teachers' attitude specifies their capability to work in order to achieve the aims and objectives of education.

Undoubtedly, attitudes depend upon school, colleagues, children, value systems, and views about life. Attitudes are

Attitude of Teachers towards Teaching

always tied up with insights and interpretations, and opinions as well as actions. An attitudinal change can be produced in a learner through teaching. Accordingly, this is interwoven with positive or negative attitude of teachers towards the pupils, the profession, classroom activities and the administration. The modern concept emphasizes on the expected behavioural outcomes. Since attitude is a psychological process, it combines beliefs, concepts, motives, values, opinions, habits and traits and has tremendous impact on pupils. Teachers with favourable attitude can successfully develop a positive attitude among children.

5.1 Significance of Attitude of Teachers

A teacher's attitude is an important variable in classroom application of new ideas and novel approaches to instruction (Reinke and Moseley, 2002). [1] Methods must be established that facilitate the development of a teacher's attitude that support contemporary instructional application of research conclusions and correspond with best practices in education (Kennedy and Kennedy, 1996). [2] Teacher education aims to produce highly motivated, conscientious and efficient classroom teachers for all levels of our educational system, and to help teachers fit into the social life of the community, and society as well. Today, the teaching profession is no longer attractive to many people as it was in the past.

In the teacher education programs, the prospective teachers' perspectives on the profession have an important place; teacher education programs have a major role to form the prospective teachers thinking towards the teaching profession. Therefore, to develop positive attitudes towards the teaching profession, the content courses and pedagogical content courses taught in teacher education program play a significant role. Celikoz and Cetin (2004) [3] opined that if prospective teachers develop a positive attitude towards their profession, they will develop creative thinking, motivate their students more easily, and would adapt to their verbal and nonverbal messages for the students. Accordingly, the prospective teacher's attitude, shaped in teacher education programs, should be encouraged to obtain a positive attitude for the teaching profession.

Research has shown that teachers who are generally unenthusiastic about the teaching profession (i.e. having a negative job orientation), are more distressed about their teaching situation than teachers who were enthusiastic (Litt and Turk 1985, p. 180). [4] Thus, for the professional growth of teachers and related developments in education, attitude held by them is very important. How a teacher performs his duty as a teacher is dependent, to a great extent, on his attitudes, values and beliefs. A positive favourable attitude makes the work not only trouble-free but also more enjoyable and professionally rewarding. A negative and unfavourable attitude makes the teaching task complicated, tedious and unpleasant. In addition, a teacher's attitude also influences the behaviour of his/her students. Thus, effectual and fruitful learning on the part of students can be achieved only by teachers with desirable attitudes.

An individual's attitude towards his profession may affect the end result. Someone who does not enjoy his work will not be able to succeed in that profession. A teacher with a positive attitude towards teaching is considered better and also becomes popular among the students. Therefore, it is very important to know the attitudes of the prospective teachers who are going to serve this noble profession of teaching. Positive attitudes not only promote learning but also create a climate which arouses effective learning. Therefore, prospective teachers must develop proper and positive attitudes towards their profession so that they can bring about a constructive change in the life of their students.

It is a fact, that teachers are generally dissatisfied in spite of the various plans and programs implemented by the state and central government from time to time. A majority of teachers do not have real love for their profession or interest in their students. The progress and standard of any nation cannot

5.2 Components of Attitude

There is an agreement among most of the social psychologists that attitude incorporates three components viz. affective, behaviour and cognitive (Carlson, 1993). [5]

5.2.1 Affective Component: This refers to the feeling and emotion one has towards an object, an act or an event which may be seemed pleasantly or unpleasantly, and that is why attitude becomes strong and dynamic.

5.2.2 Behavioural Component: Behavioural component consists of one's actions and tendencies towards an object. It is important that any particular activity a person is involved in, should be in harmony with mental tendencies to have a positive effect on the mind of an individual. This positive effect cultivates the behaviour of an individual.

5.2.3 Cognitive Component: Cognitive component of attitude consists of ideas, beliefs and understanding, which the attitude holder has about a particular object.

5.3 Characteristics of Attitude

Attitude is a complex phenomenon. Its characteristics help in unfolding its nature.

5.3.1 Attitudes are Learnt: Psychologists generally agree that attitudes are not innate; rather they are learnt and could be correlated to other aspects of learning. Freeman (1959) [6] remarked that attitudes might be said to have been learnt and become one's typical mode of response. The aspects of responses that define attitudes are the tendencies with respect to learned stimuli, identified as goal objects. The general principles of learning apply as directly to attitudes as to other behaviour such as acquisition of knowledge and skills. Guilford (1954) [7] asserted that, "The learning phenomenon of generalization and discrimination determine the lines along which attitude form and along which they function. While attitudes are subject to change, their direction and strength are sufficiently enduring over periods of time to justify treating them as personality traits". The attitudes are selectively acquired and integrated through learning and experience and they are enduring dispositions indicating response consistency. In short, all the authorities agree that attitudes are learnt and become an enduring disposition.

5.3.2 Attitudes are Learnt in a Society: Learning of attitudes occurs in a society, both formally and informally, and therefore, attitudes are culture-oriented. The process of learning of attitudes is explained as, "an important outcome of lifelong learning and maturation in interaction with the environment which is the development of the selectivity of acquired drives. As in the case of other learned responses, specific attitudes are retained as long as they are reinforced and are frequently supplanted by newly learned responses as needs and situations change" (Apple, 1983). [8]

Craft (1950) remarked that experiments provide convincing evidence that differences in past experiences bring about corresponding differences in their perceptions and their memories. Akolkar (1960) too attributed attitude formation to the influence of example, suggestibility of superiors and mass opinion. Attitude is an implicit drive producing response considered socially significant in an individual's society. Lasley (1975) [9] expressed the same viewpoint in detail. He points out that, "beliefs evolve as individuals are exposed to the ideas and more of their parents, peers, teachers, neighbours, and various others, and through the folklore of a culture, and they usually persist unmodified, unless intentionally or explicitly challenged".

All the writers quoted above express the same point of view, that attitudes are learnt by an individual through variegated forms of interaction with other individuals and social groups.

5.3.3 Attitudes are Affected by Group Norms:

Attitude of Teachers towards Teaching

Bachrach's (1972) work on auto kinetic movement contributed greatly to the social phenomenon of attitude formation and change. His work influenced a vast amount of subsequent research which led to the conclusion that one of the most important classes of factors, constituting a pressure towards conformity of attitudes and behaviour, is group norms. An individual is progressively moulded into a group's ways of seeing the auto kinetic movement, where he perceives the rate of tapping or the degree of excellence of literary passages, as they are defined for him by group participation; and that under group conditions of work, the norms and variability which had characterized the individual, when alone were rapidly forced in a direction determined by others in the group.

Attitude, judgments and other behaviours are predictable interactions reflecting identifiable personal and situational variables. In one experiment, students shifted generally from the attitudes they expressed on Thurston type attitude towards war items when they were tested alone, to clustered group expressions when they were tested in a group situation (Sharma, 1992).

Wood (1982) [10] says that when an individual is put into a group situation with others whose norms are different from one's own, the different norms tend to converge on new group norms. When individuals, new to the situation, were put into in-group, they tend to rather quickly establish a group norm that is peculiar to the group. Masan (1994), referring to the extensive laboratory research, concluded that a person is more likely to accept a group's judgment than his own when the problem is difficult. This is so, because when the other members of the group form a friendship group into which he would like to be accepted, he perceives other members as having greater expertise than himself.

These views sufficiently support the social phenomenon of learning and modification of attitude, particularly with reference to the norms of the group in which an individual happens to be placed.

62 National Education Policy (NEP), 2020 and the Role of Teachers

5.3.4 Attitudes are Inter-linked: An important aspect of attitude is its hierarchical and collateral nature within the framework of an organized and unified mental state, designated as the mental set. Mental set connotes the factors, which steer or drive volitional processes—the factors might be either conscious or unconscious. A given attitude may determine responses to a number of objects in a particular situational context and in turn be determined by the number of different prior attitudes.

Ashton and Webb (1986) [11] further pointed out that particular, minor, and often-temporary attitudes toward various objects are generally influenced by a small number of more centrally important and frequently more general major attitudes by an associative process, called subsidiation. It may be concluded that important (and usually more general) attitudes, which define a person's orientation towards life, influence more specific attitudes. Baer (1997) [12] expressed the same point of view when he remarked that attitude is oriented either by a conscious goal or by an over-ruling principle i.e. the philosophy of life. The quality of goal seeking drive of attitude was emphasized by Karathwohl (1965) [13] who argued that a tendency to respond to an object with positive or negative effect is accompanied by a cognitive structure for attaining or blocking the realization or valued states. He continued that the direction of effect, whether positive or negative with reference to the object and the strength of the effect are correlated to the content of the associated cognitive structure.

Thus, a unified and organized mental state, called mental set, is comprised of beliefs, values, likes and dislikes etc., which influence learning and modification of attitudes. Important attitudes that define a person's orientation towards life influence more specific attitudes.

5.3.5 Attitudes Determine Behaviour: The importance of attitude may be inferred from the fact that attitudes determine behaviour. Overt behaviour can be looked upon as interaction

Attitude of Teachers towards Teaching 63

reflecting the net effect of the entire structure of goal seeking drives and capabilities of an individual and the array of goals, obstacles, and detours comprising the situational setting which includes the whole life situation in terms of his expectations, perceptions, understanding and phenomenal distortions. The term interaction in this reference is important, particularly in the context of selective perceptions of an individual (Bennett, 1995).

Similarly, Case (1985) described that attitude of a subject makes a profound difference in determining which of the several possible conditioned responses will be manifest at a given time. This leads to the conclusion that attitude control behaviour through a process of selection is the repertoire of available responses. Driscoll (1994) also expresses the same point of view: "one of the most pervasive, but at the same time, most subtle effects of attitudes on behaviour, both implicit (symbolic) and overt, involves their influences on and selective modifications of the responses in a particular situational setting. These effects include both inhibition (repression) and facilitation of responses in directions consistent with the need satisfaction.

In short, attitude may be defined as a mental state, more or less enduring, representing a tendency to react favourably or unfavourably towards a designated class of stimuli. It determines behaviour and is learnt in a society through schooling, or through variegated forms of interaction with others and also through the folklore of a culture. The norms of social groups in which an individual operates and in which he likes to be accepted, modify his attitude in the direction of conformity. It is a part of an organized and unified framework of a hierarchy of attitudes, termed as mental set, in which the more basic and general attitudes affect the learning of more specific attitudes. The internalized philosophy of life has a controlling influence in the mental set, and thus influences the learning of all other attitudes. The term learning in this reference is inclusive of formation, change, modification and development. Thus, prior attitudes interact with an external situation in which a particular psychological object exists, and specific attitude towards that object is learnt or modified.

5.4 Attitude Formation

Since attitudes are not born, therefore, everyone has some individual characteristics. The environment and experiences of one's life influence these characteristics. There are several factors that influence attitude, such as domestic environment, family, socio-economic background, religious beliefs, friends, educational institutions and external environment. These factors develop an attitude towards a specific object. Attitudes are not static; they change with the passage of time, following experiences in life. The process of attitude formation takes place gradually. Padhi and Jodho (1997) found that two factors of socialization viz. social learning and personal experience are important in the formation as well as evaluation of attitude.

5.4.1 Socialization: Socialization is a process in which an individual attains harmony with the society. Understanding of the societal norms and values gradually make an individual a part of the society. This process of social learning is an integral part of growth that is usually called socialization. One has to interact with people, environment, social traditional systems and religious beliefs. This process of interaction results in an individual forming an attitude towards a specific object. Socialization is further sub-divided into conditioning and modelling (Jones and Jones, 1995).

5.4.2 Conditioning: Environmental conditions play a vital role in attitude formation. Conditioning is categorized as classical and instrumental.

Classical Conditioning: According to Lindgren and Patton (1958), [14] this is a process in which parental spanking is the unconditioned stimuli, which would automatically produce a negative or unhappy feeling in a child. If spanking is exercised overtime, a child reaches for or touches the vase. The vase will soon become a conditioned stimulus which will by itself produce a negative attitude. It is usually said that positive attitude can be produced in the same way by using an unconditioned stimuli like food which will make the child feel good. This paradigm is most relevant in the formation of evaluative feeling aspect of attitude.

Instrumental Conditioning: Instrumental conditioning is concerned with the stimulus of an individual towards a particular object. This process is called operant conditioning because in this process the organism is allowed to operate freely in an environment instead of being confined to one particular response to a particular stimulus. According to Oskamp (1977), when human behaviour is rewarded or punished for the action being taken, it is called instrumental.

Modelling or Imitation: It is quite discernible, that an individual learns through observation. One tries to follow by observing either consciously or unconsciously whomsoever she/he may consider good in manners. Parents are the best models for children. The children imitate not only the admirable but also the un-admirable behaviour of their parents. The behavioural aspects of children develop without any explicit instruction or reinforcement by parents (Irwin, 1991).

5.5 Theories of Attitude Formation

Different psychologists have explained formation of attitude according to their own theoretical perspectives. A brief introduction has been given below.

Different theories of attitude formation represent different theoretical orientations and differ primarily in the factors they emphasize upon while explaining attitude.

5.5.1 Learning Approach: Hovland and Janis (1953) see attitude as habits like anything else that is learned. Principles that apply to other forms of learning also determine the formation of attitude. Learning approach generally emphasises that attitudes are acquired from the other person through the process of social learning. Basic principles of this approach that commonly play a role in the formation of attitude are association, reinforcement and initiation. In addition to these principles, attitudes are also formed as a result of direct personal experiences (Baron and Byrne. 1993).

5.5.2 Motivational Theories: Incentive theory holds that a person adopts an attitude which maximizes his/her gains. According to Heider's (1958) theory, the similarity attraction effect is generated by the tendency to maintain a coherence or balance one's perceptions regarding the objects of common concern.

5.5.3 Cognitive-affective Consistency Theory: Rosenberg (1960) emphasizes that people try to make their cognition consistent with their effects. This theory asserts that our evaluations influence our beliefs.

Festinger (1957) proposed the dissonance theory, focused on two principles of attitude-behaviour inconsistency: (a) the effects of making decision, and (b) the effects of engaging in counter attitudinal behaviour.

5.5.4 Self-perception Theory: It describes that our attitudes are based simply on perceptions of our own behaviour and/or circumstances in which the behaviour occurs.

Craft (1950) noted that experiments provide evidence that perception is influenced by an individual's attitude towards his own place in the social environment and by ideas of prestige and the intensity of need towards the object perceived. Borich (1977) reported results of a study about teacher attitude and perception. Teachers with more positive attitudes towards teaching and higher aspirations for achievement in teaching and with longer time commitments to teaching generally perceived their principles more positively. They also perceived students as more potentially autonomous and had more positive views about their students. Morrison (1976) reported Gough's (1953) study wherein significant differences between white and black teachers in attitude towards pupils of both races from low-income families were found. White teachers described them as talkative, lazy, high-strung and rebellious and blamed parents and children for teaching problems whereas black teachers described them as happy, cooperative energetic and ambitious and blamed the physical environment for problems.

The obvious conclusion from the above studies is that attitude about an object is influenced by the perception of an individual towards self and social environment and ideas of prestige. Perception is influenced by attitude.

5.6 Teacher Training and Attitudes

One of the concerns of teacher training is to bring about changes in attitude. Lortie (1975), [15] remarked that in the realm of attitude change, teacher training is concerned with desirable changes in student-teacher attitude. Teacher training programs in general also contribute in shaping teacher's attitudes. Several studies have reported positive changes in the attitudes of teachers as a result of educational courses. In one study, significant positive changes were reported with regards to expansion and reorganization of curriculum, formal discipline, recognition of individual differences and personality development. In other studies, significant changes towards more positive attitudes were observed as a result of theory courses in education.

Morrison (1976) reported the results of one of the most thorough and extensive investigation. He found marked changes in both educational and social attitude, especially the changes towards greater social radicalism and educational naturalism and away from educational formalism and a trend away from religious values toward more utilitarian values. All these changes were in the direction of attitudes held by a majority of lecturers in the colleges.

Dunham (1959) reported that mostly significant changes in positive direction were registered during the theory courses. Changes in attitude during the practice teaching tended to approximate with the attitude held by college supervisors or supervising teachers, under whom the practice teaching was completed. Cross (1960) reported significant positive gains in attitudes of teachers during the method courses and during student teaching. The changes generally were in the direction of attitudes held by instructors and supervisors. Osman (1959) reported different results about changes in attitude. He reported significant loss in pre- and post-test mean scores during student teaching. The students who had gained in scores reported the teaching experience as very satisfactory, and those who had lost, reported it as unsatisfactory.

Hogben (1979) [16] remarked that evidence suggests that impact of formal teacher education and theory in particular on attitudes is real. Person (1998) found that teachers with little or no training used restriction more often than indirect guidance. Certified teachers who had a great deal of training showed most concern with the child getting along with his peers and being considerate to the rights and feelings of others. These teachers were less concerned about control and restraint. As the teacher's amount of training increased, their attitude towards authority became less arbitrary and the attitude of warmth increased.

Research evidence as presented above, suggests that teacher education programs generally achieve the objective of bringing about positive changes in the attitude of student teachers toward teaching, particularly by theory courses. The change, or at least part of it, is carried over to teaching situations, wherein it is significant when compared to untrained teachers.

The quantitative expansion of secondary education has resulted in dilution of quality as regards selection of teachers and programs of teacher training are concerned. As remedy to this, improving the knowledge and teaching competence of teachers and inculcating them with healthy professional attitude and desirable teacher like qualities is necessary. For the professional preparation of teachers, the study of attitudes is very important. How a teacher performs his duty is paramount, since a teacher, is dependent to a great extent, on his attitudes, values, and beliefs. Positive attitude towards teaching as a profession and towards teaching per se has been

Attitude of Teachers towards Teaching 69

recognized as important characteristics of an effective teacher. Different studies on teacher effectiveness have established the fact that teacher attitude and teacher effectiveness are positively correlated.

It is true that some professionals are driven by passionate interest in their work. They show a deep level of enjoyment and involvement in what they do (Hunt, 1990). Theorists call passion for a profession as a deep task involvement and elation (Clifford, 1999). [17] This background gives us the theoretical assumption, which has led to posit that stable personality characteristics seem to be essential for the teaching profession.

Endnotes

1. Reinke, K. and Moseley, C. (2002), "The Effects of Teacher Education on Elementary and Secondary Pre-service Teacher's Belief about Integration: A Longitudinal Study", *Action in Teacher Education*, 24, 31-39.

2. Kenndy, C. and Kenndy, J. (1996), "Teacher Attitudes and Change Implementation", *System*, 24, 351-360.

3. Celikoz, N. and Cetin, F. (2004), "Anatohan Teacher High School Students' Attitude about the Factors Affecting the Teaching Profession", *National Education Journal*, 162, 234-241.

4. Litt, M.D. and Turk, D.C. (1985), "Sources of Stress and Dissatisfaction in Experienced High School Teachers", *Journal of Educational Research*, 78, 3, 178-185.

5. Carlson, E.R. (1956), "Attitude Change through Modification of Attitude Structure", *Journal of Abnormal and Social Psychology*, 52, 256-261.

6. Freeman, Frank S. (1959), "Theory of Practice of Psychological Testing", 484.

7. Guilford, (1954), "Psychometric Methods", McGraw-Hill Book Company, New York.

8. Apple, M.W. (1983), "Work, Gender and Teachers College Record", 84(3), 611-628.

9. Lasely, Thomas J. (1975), "Pre-service Teacher Beliefs about Teaching", *Journal of Teacher Education*, 31, (4), 38.

10. Wood, W. (1982), "Access to Attitude-relevant Information in Memory as a Determinant of Persuasion: The Role of Message

Attributes", *Journal of Experimental Social Psychology*, 21, 73-85.

11. Ashton, P.T. and Webb, R.B. (1986), "Making a Difference: Teachers' Sense of Efficacy and Student Achievement", New York: Longman.

12. Baer, J. (1997), "Creative Teachers, Creative Students", Boston: Allyn and Bacon.

13. Krathwohl, David (1964), "Taxonomy of Educational Objectives: Handbook 2", New York: David McKay.

14. Lindgren, H.C. and Patton, G.M. (1958), 'Opinionnaire on Attitudes towards Education", 80-83.

15. Lortie, D. (1975), "School Teacher: A Sociological Study", London: University of Chicago Press.

16. Hogben, D. and Petty, M. (1979), "Early Changes in Teacher Attitude", *Educational Research*, 212-219.

17. Clifford, S. Zimmerman (1999), "Thinking beyond My Own Interpretations: Reflections on Collaborative and Cooperative Learning Theory in the Law School Curriculum", available at: http://www.teachersatrisk.com/2008/08/06/a-positive-attittude-is-key-to-maintaining-a-positive-classroom-climate/#sthash.KaQVZ6gl.dpuf.

6

Attitude of Prospective Teachers towards Teaching Profession: A Research-based Case Study

This case study pertains to the attitude of prospective teachers towards the teaching profession studying in teacher training colleges affiliated to the C.C.S. University, Meerut, located in Ghaziabad district of Uttar Pradesh.

The study was conducted on a sample of 590 prospective teachers. Random sampling method was applied for selecting the sample of colleges and stratified random sampling method for selecting the prospective teachers as samples for the study. After a detailed study of all these methods and considering the variables selected for the research work, the stratified sampling method was found to be the most suitable one. Out of 590 prospective teachers, 290 were male and 300 were female prospective teachers. Further, area-wise, there were 285 urban and 305 rural prospective teachers in the sample. Moreover, out of 590 prospective teachers, 289 were from the science stream and 311 from the arts stream. Additionally, of 590 prospective teachers, 304 were graduates and 296 were post-graduate.

Finally, 20 prospective teachers were selected for the case study with an extremely high and an extremely low teacher attitude scores. These 20 prospective teachers were interviewed though a self-designed interview schedule.

6.1 Teacher as a Dynamic Force of an Institution

A teacher is the real and dynamic force of any institution. The school without him/her is a sole less body. Without good, devoted and competent teachers, even the best system is bound

72 National Education Policy (NEP), 2020 and the Role of Teachers

to fail. A good teacher can certainly derive best results even out of the worst system. He/she is a powerful and abiding influence in the formation of character; the influence of a great teacher indirectly extends over many generations.

Teacher is a benchmark that measures the achievements and aspirations of a nation. The worth and potentiality of a country is evaluated by the work of teachers. People of a nation are the distended replications of their teacher. The role played by teachers becomes a very important component and in fact it can be said that they are the real nation-builders. Teachers work in close co-ordination with students to help them in building up their future. They mould the students to bring out their skills or improvise them, teaching good habits/attitudes and helping them become good citizens of a nation. Teaching is one of the most complicated jobs today. It demands broad knowledge of a subject matter, curriculum, and standards, enthusiasm, caring attitude, love of learning, knowledge of discipline and classroom management techniques, and a desire to make a difference in the lives of young people. With all these qualities required, it is no wonder that it is hard to find great teachers.

Primarily, excellent and efficient teachers can change the fate of the nation. It is in schools, colleges and universities that the development of attitudes and dispositions necessary for a progressive life in the society, takes place. Since education is imparted by teachers, if a teacher is capable, energetic, mentally strong and having a positive attitude, it is good for the institution. A teacher helps a child in bringing out the hidden capabilities. He/she unfolds what is within, hidden and untapped. He/she makes explicit what is implicit in the students. Hence, teachers' importance in teaching-learning process is very primal.

6.2 Behaviour of Teacher in a Classroom

Teaching being an interactive process, it has now been realized that a teacher's behaviour in a classroom is chiefly responsible for the proper educational growth of pupils.

Teaching is often called a calling, not a profession or a trade or simply a job. This means that a teacher should regard himself/herself as one, specially called to do this work, not so much for the pecuniary benefits which he/she may derive from it as for the love of it. The teacher must possess a strong sense of line of work, true devotion and a positive attitude towards teaching. The strength of a school depends on the attitude of its teachers. For qualitative improvement in secondary education of our country, selection of right type of prospective teachers is a must.

This requires not only improving the knowledge and teaching competence of prospective teachers but also inculcating in them, healthy professional attitudes and desirable teacher like qualities. Therefore, securing the right type of prospective teachers for training is very important. Unless such prospective teachers are found, our secondary schools won't be able to deliver as per our expectations. Therefore, for the professional preparation of prospective teachers, the study of attitudes held by them is very important. A positive favourable attitude makes the work not only easier but also more satisfying and professionally rewarding. A negative or unfavourable attitude makes the teaching task harder, more tedious and unpleasant.

The effectiveness of the process of education has been squarely acknowledged to depend upon the teaching attitude of teachers. It may not be considered in anyway an exaggerated statement that it is the teaching attitude of the teachers that is primarily perceived as the effectiveness of any system of education. This leads one to enunciate that teachers' attitude specifies their capability to work for the achievement of the aims and objectives of education.

The role of a teacher in the educational process is always challenging and vibrant. A teacher's task is not only to spread knowledge rather it is something more. The greatest of the tasks of a teacher is to inspire and motivate students towards the exquisite goals. A teacher in a naturalistic set up is only a setter of the stage, a supplier of material and opportunities, a provider of an ideal environment, and a creator of conditions under which natural development takes place. Teaching is a core profession and a key agent of change in today's knowledge society. Issue of teacher quality, training and continuous professional development is vital for the improvement of not only our education system but also in achieving the goals of education.

Research has shown that teachers who are generally unenthusiastic about the teaching profession (i.e. having a negative job orientation), are more distressed about their teaching situation compared to teachers who were enthusiastic (Litt and Turk 1985, p. 180). Thus, for the professional growth of the teachers and developments in education, attitudes held by them are very important. How a teacher performs his/her duty as a teacher is dependent to a great extent on his attitudes, values and beliefs. A positive favourable attitude makes the work not only trouble-free but also more enjoyable and professionally rewarding. A negative and unfavourable attitude makes a teaching task complicated, tedious and unpleasant. In addition, a teacher's attitude also influences the behaviour of his/her students. Thus, effectual and fruitful learning on the part of students can be achieved only by teachers with desirable attitudes.

An individual's attitude towards his profession may affect the end result. Someone who does not enjoy his work will not be able to succeed in that profession. A teacher with a positive attitude towards teaching is considered better and becomes popular among the students. Therefore, it is very important to know the attitudes of the prospective teachers who are going to serve this noble profession of teaching. Positive attitudes not only promote learning but also create the climate which arouses an effective learning. Therefore, prospective teachers must develop proper and positive attitudes towards their profession so that they can bring about a constructive change in the life of their students.

6.3 Dissatisfied Teachers

It is a fact, that a majority of teachers are really dissatisfied in spite of the various plans and programs having been implemented by the state and central governments. Quite a number of teachers have no real love for their profession or interest in their students. The progress and standard of any nation cannot be beyond the standard of its system of education and the standard of educational institutions. The standard of any educational institution, in turn, cannot rise beyond the levels of its teachers. Naturally, the question arises: what is the real situation? Do the teachers really have unfavourable attitude towards the teaching profession? Is teacher attitude influenced by gender, locale, stream and educational qualifications etc.? In order to get the answer to the above questions, the researchers decided to take up a systematic and objective attitudinal study of the prospective teachers towards the teaching profession, classroom teaching, child-cantered practices, educational process, pupils and teachers with special reference to their sex, locale, stream and educational qualifications.

Teaching has been one of the oldest and respected professions in the world. The role, functions, competence and preparation of teachers has undergone a dramatic change from time to time but the need for teachers has been imperative at all times. The changing times as well as the requirements of the society have necessitated changes in the ways teacher preparation is done.

A teacher training program can offer precious insights and information about the previous teachers. These educational experiences have made a difference in their lives, and for whatever reasons, they are now taking into consideration a career in teaching. For the undergraduate students who continue and receive a degree in teaching, it will be important for them to always remember how it felt to be like a student and share with their students that there is no greater wisdom than kindness. Many prospective teachers join this profession not by choice but by chance or due to other reasons. They are not interested in opting for this profession. They just choose teaching profession as a second choice, in case they fail to succeed in their first choice. They are generally frustrated throughout the training period.

Positive attitude is an important aspect for success in the teaching profession. It should be the aim of any teacher education program to produce pre-service teachers who can start their career with positive attitudes towards the teaching profession. As we know, teaching profession plays a vital role in the overall development of a nation. Therefore, it is very essential to explore the attitude of B.Ed students who would be the future teachers of the country. A teacher's positive attitude does cause a sequence reaction of positive thoughts, events and outcomes.

A teacher's positive attitude is a means and ignites extraordinary results. If the teachers are well-trained and highly motivated, learning will be enhanced. Teaching profession demands a clear set of goals, love for profession and obviously a more favourable attitude towards the profession. Effective attitudes and actions employed by teachers can ultimately make a positive difference in the lives of students.

There is always a need to evaluate the efforts which are being made by the training institutions to achieve the desired results. It is highly documented that healthy attitude towards teaching, contributes to successful teaching. Hence, there is a great need for the study of teacher attitude of prospective teachers in relation to their gender, locality, stream and educational qualifications. Consequently, the researchers feel that prospective teacher's opinions or their attitudes can never be ignored, rather those should be reviewed or re-explored from time to time and it is this feeling that urged this investigator to take up the present study of a particular region viz. Ghaziabad district of Uttar Pradesh.

6.4 Major Findings of the Study

The major findings of the study obtained following analysis of the data, are presented below:

1. It was found that female prospective teachers felt more comfortable and secure in teaching profession. They could easily fulfil their family responsibilities along with the profession.

2. Unfavourable attitude towards the teaching profession was found in prospective male teachers. They took teaching as a profession because it was easy for them to get employment in this profession and also their low grades did not provide them the opportunity to secure a place in other courses.

3. Urban prospective teachers wanted to bring about a change in the field of education by interacting with the students and providing them the desired knowledge with the help of new techniques. They were satisfied with the basic amenities which a teaching job provided them.

4. Rural prospective teachers were found with a very negative attitude towards the teaching profession because of low pay scale, ineffective government policies, and unsatisfying working conditions.

5. It was found that prospective teachers differed according to the gender, with reference to their teaching attitude. Among all prospective teachers, females had a more positive attitude towards the teaching profession. This finding can be interpreted as an indicator of the fact that compared to the past, teaching profession is gradually becoming a profession for the female community per se. Therefore, it is recommended that sensitization workshops and seminars, especially for prospective male teachers, should be organised for developing their positive attitude towards the teaching profession.

6. Urban prospective teachers had greater positive attitudes than rural prospective teachers towards the profession of teaching. Accordingly, it is recommended, that an

enhanced infrastructure, satisfying working conditions, and adequate recourses should be provided so that people who belong to rural areas get motivated to join this profession.

7. Female prospective teachers had a more favourable attitude towards the teaching profession, classroom teaching, child-cantered practices, and educational processes compared to male prospective teachers.

8. Urban prospective teachers had a higher attitude towards the teaching profession, classroom teaching, educational processes and pupils, compared to rural prospective teachers. Simultaneously, urban prospective teachers and rural prospective teachers had same attitude towards child-cantered practices.

9. Science prospective teachers and arts prospective teachers were similar in terms of attitude towards the teaching profession, classroom teaching, child-cantered practices, educational processes, and pupils.

10. Post-graduate prospective teachers had a more favourable attitude towards the classroom teaching than the graduate prospective teachers. No difference was found in the attitude towards the teaching profession, child-cantered practices, educational processes, and pupils.

6.5 Conclusions

Attitudes involve some knowledge of a situation and play an important role in determining one's personality. Teacher's attitudes not only affect their behaviour in the classroom but also influence the behaviour of their students. On the basis of the analysis of the data collected through questionnaire and interviews the following conclusions can be drawn.

On the basis of the results of the case study, it was observed that female prospective teachers considered teaching as the best career option since they could devote sufficient time to both their personal and professional lives. Their family members did not object to it, apart from being considered a respectable profession in the society.

On the other hand, male prospective teachers harboured prejudice towards the teaching profession and usually opted for it owing to the lack of other available career options. They wanted to involve themselves in other occupations for the reason of earning more money. They were not fully devoted towards the teaching profession. There were many factors which contributed towards the negative attitude of male prospective teachers towards the teaching profession. These included insufficient salaries, poor working conditions, low morale, lack of job satisfaction, lack of opportunities and inability to support their families. Furthermore, public attitude towards the teaching profession was not optimistic regards males compared to its suitability for the female counterparts.

As far as locale of the prospective teachers was concerned, the researcher arrived at the conclusion that urban prospective teachers were more positive and better placed in this profession rather than the rural ones. Most of the urban teachers were found modern in their thinking. They considered it as the best profession to serve their nation while sharing knowledge with the others. They wanted to involve electronic media and computer technology in teaching as well as develop new methodologies, innovations, and techniques of teaching. They considered it a very challenging job and were ready to face all the challenges positively.

On the other hand, it was found that rural prospective teachers choose this profession following their failure to find openings in any other profession. It was also discovered that teaching professionals in rural areas were not in sync with the latest technology due to lack of resources, facilities, etc. This in turn created a dismal image in the minds of prospective teachers who were clearly not motivated enough to engage in this profession. After analyzing the results, it can be concluded that locale and gender domain does affect teacher attitude significantly.

It is well known, that teaching is visualized as a powerful

tool in bringing about changes in everyday sphere of our life. The whole process of education is done through a personality known as a teacher. Only well-trained and highly motivated teachers can boost the teaching-learning process. Teaching is a dignified and challenging profession and it is important to note that those teachers can better perform, who are sufficiently prepared and have a strong professional attitude.

If a teacher is completely satisfied by the profession, the students will also show a positive attitude towards the teaching profession as such. College managements and governments also have to provide good infrastructure and institutional facilities to the prospective teachers. Quality education should be given to the prospective teachers by well qualified teacher educators. If all the facilities are good, automatically the attitude towards the teaching profession will be favourable for the prospective teachers. It is pertinent, that people engaged in this profession should follow the value system with purity and dedication.

On the basis of this study, we can say that prospective teachers with a positive attitude perform better in teaching and learning process. They are more motivated towards their profession. They are punctual and respect their colleagues also. In this study, it was also found that prospective teachers with a positive attitude have a helpful behaviour towards students, parents and their colleagues.

6.6 Educational Implications

The findings of the present investigation may be helpful for teachers, students, parents, principals, research scholars, recruiting authorities, policy makers and curriculum developers.

The findings of the study may provide a helping hand to students so that they may choose this profession while maintaining a positive attitude. They should not follow the pre-determined path of others and should rather try to make their own path while embarking upon any career. An individual's choice of occupation depends not only on his own characteristics but on those also, which are perceived best for the occupation as well.

Research scholars of education and psychology can also benefit by the findings of the present study. Findings of the present study would serve as a basic data for further studies related to attitude of prospective teachers.

Findings of the present study will also provide feedback to policy makers and authorities concerned regards the prospective teachers. The findings would be instrumental in laying down policies for prospective teachers who have a better teacher attitude.

Principals of the institutions would also be benefited by the findings of the study in terms of making improvements in attitude towards teaching. Seminars, lectures, sensitization workshops and teleconferences should be frequently organized for generating positive attitudes towards the teaching profession. Through this, one can increase the devotion and dedication of teachers towards their institution which will ultimately work as a measure of quality improvement in secondary teacher training.

The findings of the study would also prove beneficial for teacher trainees as they are the future teachers and should develop a favourable attitude towards the teaching profession and attain mastery over the methods of creative teaching. They will be in a position to take up initiatives for the improvement of the overall environment of their schools. Individual and group counselling should also be carried out in motivating and developing positive attitudes towards the teaching profession among the prospective teachers.

In a nutshell, it may be said that teacher attitude is extremely important because of the relationship that exists between attitude and action. There exists scores of studies reporting an association between low morale, lack of job satisfaction, inadequate working conditions, lack of motivation, and lack of confidence in the teaching profession.

The responsibility lies with the educators to build a positive attitude amongst the prospective teachers regards the teaching profession, since they are the most important element in the educational process. By doing so, teachers will be more effective in their jobs which would be translated into specific classroom and instructional practices which in turn would improve the student behaviour and learning outcomes.

6.7 Suggestions for Further Research

The results of this study provide several directions for future researches. This study has specifically examined the attitude of prospective teachers with special reference to their sex, locale, stream and educational qualifications towards the teaching profession, classroom teaching, child centred practices, educational processes, and pupils. In the light of above mentioned implications for education, following suggestions are extended, as outlined below:

1. This study suggests that attitude of teachers towards the teaching profession must also be tested on the basis of other variables, like personality, intelligence, creativity, teaching competency, teaching aptitude, achievement motivation, level of aspiration, caste etc. It is also recommended that such type of study must be investigated outside the Ghaziabad district for its rationality.

2. A similar study can also be conducted at the primary, secondary and higher levels in India.

3. Comparative surveys on this problem can be undertaken in different states of India.

4. Some studies can be carried out in other varied fields of education viz. technical, medical and engineering.

5. The attitude of the prospective school teachers belonging to different socio-economic strata may be investigated.

6. The study can be repeated on a large sample for getting more reliable and valid results.

7. A study of teacher attitude may be conducted with respect to the medium of instruction.

Attitude of Prospective Teachers towards Teaching Profession... 83

8. Causal studies may be undertaken to assess the reasons behind favourable and unfavourable attitude of the prospective teachers.

While summing up, we would like to acknowledge the fact that a scientific endeavour in any field of study is an ongoing process. Hence, we do not propose to claim any finality in regard to either the facts gathered or the inferences drawn. The present study in its own limited way has, however, made its contribution towards the process of building up a solid knowledge base regarding the teaching profession. If it succeeds in provoking further research in the field, the efforts would be fructified.

The real success of qualitative improvement in teacher training depends upon the sense of purpose, devotion and commitment of teachers who feel proud of the teaching profession. Sensitization workshops and seminars should be organized for parents and guardians to advocate the importance of allowing their children and wards to enrol in the teacher education programmes. Career guidance should be intensified right from the primary school level with special preference for building positive attitudes among the students towards the teaching profession.

Courses and activities that will prepare the prospective teachers for their profession should be increased in teacher training colleges along with individual and group counselling, which would help in motivating and developing positive attitudes towards the teaching profession.

It is expected that this study, though small, would be able to make valuable contribution in the field of education. The investigators strongly believe that a study of attitudes of prospective teachers and its association will be much helpful in identifying factors that preside over the behaviour of prospective teachers. It will also be useful in developing the extrapolative measures that can be employed during the selection of candidates for teacher training programmes. The study should bring about an extensive change in the attitudes

84　National Education Policy (NEP), 2020 and the Role of Teachers

of prospective teacher community towards teaching. The results of the study would also be helpful for the future students who want to join the teaching profession and for the parents too, to decide about teaching as profession for their children. Teachers would also be able to correlate with the findings so as to prepare their students to join this profession.

7

Education, Women Empowerment and Literacy Rates

India has to provide quality education and develop the skills of its large young population to fully reap the benefits of the demographic dividend. Currently, many programmes are being implemented both in elementary and secondary education and higher and technical education.

Education has been a thrust sector ever since India attained Independence in 1947. Right from the inception of planning, the crucial role of education in economic and social development has been recognised and emphasised. Efforts to increase people's participation in education and to diversify educational programmes in order to promote knowledge and skills required for nation-building have characterised successive Five Year Plans. Despite a series of problems that the country faced soon after independence, it has been possible to create a vast educational infrastructure in terms of large enrolments and teaching force and massive capabilities for management, research and development.

7.1 Education and Human Potential

Education is fundamental for achieving full human potential, developing an equitable and just society, and promoting national development. Providing universal access to quality education is the key to India's continued ascent, and leadership on the global stage in terms of economic growth, social justice and equality, scientific advancement, national integration, and cultural preservation. Universal high-quality education is the best way forward for developing and maximizing our country's rich talents and resources for the good of the individual, the society, the country, and the world. India will have the highest population of young people in the world over the next decade, and our ability to provide high-quality educational opportunities to them will determine the future of our country.

According to National Education Policy (NEP), 2020, "The world is undergoing rapid changes in the knowledge landscape. With various dramatic scientific and technological advances, such as the rise of big data, machine learning, and artificial intelligence, many unskilled jobs worldwide may be taken over by machines, while the need for a skilled workforce, particularly involving mathematics, computer science, and data science, in conjunction with multi-disciplinary abilities across the sciences, social sciences, and humanities, will be increasingly in greater demand. With climate change, increasing pollution, and depleting natural resources, there will be a sizeable shift in how we meet the world's energy, water, food, and sanitation needs, again resulting in the need for new skilled labour, particularly in biology, chemistry, physics, agriculture, climate science, and social science.

The growing emergence of epidemics and pandemics will also call for collaborative research in infectious disease management and development of vaccines and the resultant social issues heightens the need for multidisciplinary learning. There will be a growing demand for humanities and arts, as India moves towards becoming a developed country as well as among the three largest economies in the world". [1]

Indeed, with the quickly changing employment landscape and global ecosystem, it is becoming increasingly critical that children not only learn, but more importantly learn how to learn. Education thus, must move towards less content, and more towards learning about how to think critically and solve problems, how to be creative and multidisciplinary, and how to innovate, adapt, and absorb new material in novel and changing fields. Pedagogy must evolve to make education

Education, Women Empowerment and Literacy Rates   87

more experiential, holistic, integrated, inquiry-driven, discovery-oriented, learner-centred, discussion-based, flexible, and, of course, enjoyable.

The curriculum must include basic arts, crafts, humanities, games, sports and fitness, languages, literature, culture, and values, in addition to science and mathematics, to develop all aspects and capabilities of learners; and make education more well-rounded, useful, and fulfilling to the learner. Education must build character, enable learners to be ethical, rational, compassionate, and caring, while at the same time prepare them for gainful, fulfilling employment.

The gap between the current state of learning outcomes and what is required must be bridged through undertaking major reforms that bring the highest quality, equity, and integrity into the system, from early childhood care and education through higher education.

The aim must be for India to have an education system by 2040 that is second to none, with equitable access to the highest-quality education for all learners regardless of social or economic background.

Education policy must provide to all students, irrespective of their place of residence, a quality education system, with particular focus on historically marginalized, disadvantaged, and underrepresented groups. Education is a great leveller and is the best tool for achieving economic and social mobility, inclusion, and equality. Initiatives must be in place to ensure that all students from such groups, despite inherent obstacles, are provided various targeted opportunities to enter and excel in the educational system.

These elements must be incorporated taking into account the local and global needs of the country, and with a respect for and deference to its rich diversity and culture. Instilling knowledge of India and its varied social, cultural, and technological needs, its inimitable artistic, language, and knowledge traditions, and its strong ethics in India's young people is considered critical for purposes of national pride,

88 National Education Policy (NEP), 2020 and the Role of Teachers

self-confidence, self-knowledge, cooperation, and integration.

The purpose of the education system is to develop good human beings capable of rational thought and action, possessing compassion and empathy, courage and resilience, scientific temper and creative imagination, with sound ethical moorings and values. It should aim at producing engaged, productive, and contributing citizens for building an equitable, inclusive, and plural society as envisaged by our Constitution. A good education institution is one in which every student feels welcomed and cared for, where a safe and stimulating learning environment exists, where a wide range of learning experiences are offered, and where good physical infrastructure and appropriate resources conducive to learning are available to all students. Attaining these qualities must be the goal of every educational institution. However, at the same time, there must also be seamless integration and coordination across institutions and across all stages of education.

Education is the single greatest tool for achieving social justice and equality. Inclusive and equitable education, while indeed an essential goal in its own right, is also critical to achieving an inclusive and equitable society in which every citizen has the opportunity to dream, thrive, and contribute to the nation. The education system must aim to benefit India's children so that no child loses any opportunity to learn and excel because of circumstances of birth or background. This Policy reaffirms that bridging the social category gaps in access, participation, and learning outcomes in school education will continue to be one of the major goals of all education sector development programmes.

There are innate talents in every student, which must be discovered, nurtured, fostered, and developed. These talents may express themselves in the form of varying interests, dispositions, and capacities. Those students that show particularly strong interests and capacities in a given realm must be encouraged to pursue that realm beyond the general school curriculum.

Education, Women Empowerment and Literacy Rates 89

Underscoring the importance of education and the needed focus on it, the Twelfth Five Year Plan (2012-17) stated, "Education is the most important lever for social, economic and political transformation. A well-educated population, equipped with the relevant knowledge, attitudes and skills is essential for economic and social development in the twenty-first century. Education is the most potent tool for socio-economic mobility and a key instrument for building an equitable and just society. Education provides skills and competencies for economic well-being. Education strengthens democracy by imparting to citizens the tools needed to fully participate in the governance process. Education also acts as an integrative force in society, imparting values that foster social cohesion and national identity. Recognising the importance of education in national development, the Twelfth Plan places an unprecedented focus on the expansion of education, on significantly improving the quality of education imparted and on ensuring that educational opportunities are available to all segments of the society". [2]

7.2 Education in Ancient India

According to National Education Policy (NEP), 2020, "The pursuit of knowledge (Jnan), wisdom (Pragyaa), and truth (Satya) was always considered in Indian thought and philosophy as the highest human goal. The aim of education in ancient India was not just the acquisition of knowledge as preparation for life in this world, or life beyond schooling, but for the complete realization and liberation of the self. World-class institutions of ancient India such as Takshashila, Nalanda, Vikramshila, Vallabhi, set the highest standards of multidisciplinary teaching and research and hosted scholars and students from across backgrounds and countries. The Indian education system produced great scholars such as Charaka, Susruta, Aryabhata, Varahamihira, Bhaskaracharya, Brahmagupta, Chanakya, Chakrapani Datta, Madhava, Panini, Patanjali, Nagarjuna, Gautama, Pingala, Sankardev, Maitreyi, Gargi and Thiruvalluvar, among numerous others, who made seminal contributions to world knowledge in diverse fields such as mathematics, astronomy, metallurgy, medical science and surgery, civil engineering, architecture, shipbuilding and navigation, yoga, fine arts, chess, and more. Indian culture and philosophy have had a strong influence on the world. These rich legacies to world heritage must not only be nurtured and preserved for posterity but also researched, enhanced, and put to new uses through our education system". [3]

NEP, 2020 further states, "India has a long tradition of holistic and multidisciplinary learning, from universities such as Takshashila and Nalanda, to the extensive literatures of India combining subjects across fields. Ancient Indian literary works such as Banabhatta's Kadambari described a good education as knowledge of the 64 Kalaas or arts; and among these 64 'arts' were not only subjects, such as singing and painting, but also 'scientific' fields, such as chemistry and mathematics, 'vocational' fields such as carpentry and clothes-making, 'professional' fields, such as medicine and engineering, as well as 'soft skills' such as communication, discussion, and debate. The very idea that all branches of creative human endeavour, including mathematics, science, vocational subjects, professional subjects, and soft skills should be considered 'arts', has distinctly Indian origins. This notion of a 'knowledge of many arts' or what in modern times is often called the 'liberal arts' (i.e., a liberal notion of the arts) must be brought back to Indian education, as it is exactly the kind of education that will be required for the 21st century". [4]

7.3 Constitutional Provisions Regarding Education

Vide Entry 25 of List III (Concurrent List) in the Seventh Schedule of the Constitution of India, education is a concurrent subject and hence a subject of common interest to both the Central and State Governments.

In a historic move, the Constitution (Eighty-sixth Amendment) Act, 2002, amended the Constitution by inserting Article 21A which reads as follows: "The State shall provide free and compulsory education to all children of the age of six to fourteen years in such manner as the State may, by law, determine." This was a significant measure for achieving the goal of Education for All (EFA) by making free and compulsory elementary education a fundamental right for all children in the age group of 6-14 years.

Again, the year 2010 was a landmark for education in India as the Right of Children to Free and Compulsory Education (RTE), Act, 2009 was enforced with effect from April 1, 2010. RTE Act, 2009, representing the consequential legislation to the Constitution (Eighty-sixth Amendment) Act, 2002, secures the right of children to free and compulsory education till completion of elementary education in a neighbourhood school. RTE Act, 2009 lays down norms and standards relating to pupil teacher ratios, buildings and infrastructure, school working days and working hours of teachers.

In order to fulfil the constitutional obligation, *Sarva Shiksha Abhiyan* was launched in partnership with the States. The programme is an effort towards recognition of the need for improving the performance of the school system through a community-owned approach and ensuring quality elementary education in a mission mode to all children in the age group of 6-14 years by 2010. It also seeks to bridge gender and social gaps. This programme subsumed all existing programmes (except *Mahila Samakhya* and Mid-day Meal Schemes) including externally-aided programmes with its overall framework with district as the unit of programmes implementation.

7.4 Role of Education in the Development Process

Education is the most crucial investment in human development. Education strongly influences improvement in health, hygiene, demographic profile, productivity and practically all that is connected with the quality of life. Education is important in the development process for two reasons. First, because education can be viewed as an end in itself as it improves the perception of life of people. Secondly, education leads to formation of human capital and is an important investment for the development process.

Education is the catalytic factor which leads to human resource development comprising better health and nutrition, improved socio-economic opportunities and more congenial and beneficial natural environment for all. There is already enough evidence in India to show that high literacy rates, especially high female literacy rates, are associated with low rates of population growth, infant mortality and maternal mortality besides a higher rate of life expectancy.

Human resources development has necessarily to be assigned a key role in any development strategy, particularly in a country with a large population. Trained and educated on sound lines, a large population can itself become an asset in accelerating economic growth and in ensuring social change in desired directions. Education develops basic skills and abilities and fosters a value system conducive to, and in support of, national development goals, both long-term and immediate. In a world where knowledge is increasing at an exponential rate, the task of education in the diffusion of new knowledge and, at the same time, in the preservation and promotion of what is basic to India's culture and ethos, is both complex and challenging.

The system of education has a determining influence on the rate at which economic progress is achieved and the benefits which can be derived from it. Economic development naturally makes growing demands on human resources and in a democratic set up it calls for values and attitudes in the building up of which the quality of education is an important element.

Education is of basic importance in the planned development of a nation. The educational machinery has to be geared for the specific tasks which the nation sets itself so as to make available, in the various fields, personnel of suitable quality at the required rate. The educational system has also an intimate bearing on the attainment of general objectives of social policy as it largely determines the quality of the

Education, Women Empowerment and Literacy Rates 93

manpower and the social climate of the community.

7.5 Objectives of Education Policy

The Resolution on the National Policy on Education adopted in 1968 pointed out that the great leaders of the Indian freedom movement realised the fundamental role of education and—throughout the struggle for independence—stressed the unique significance of education for national development. The Resolution further declared that the radical re-construction of education should involve the following:

1. Transformation of the system to relate it more closely to the life of the people.
2. Continuous effort to expand educational opportunity.
3. Sustained and intensive effort to raise the quality of education at all stages.
4. Emphasis on the development of science and technology.
5. Cultivation of moral and social values.

According to the Resolution, the educational system must produce young men and women of character and ability, committed to national service and development.

In a democratic set up, the role of education becomes crucial, since it can function effectively only if there is an intelligent participation of the masses in the affairs of the country.

Education, broadly perceived as a seamless continuum of life-long learning, is essential for human resource development at every age level. In a package of developmental inputs available to the community, education should form an effective means to: (a) improve the status and character of living patterns of the people, (b) help intellectual, social and emotional development of the individuals, (c) enable them to meet their basic needs of daily life, (d) satisfy cultural needs which are essential for the healthy growth of a nation and (e) stimulate the growth of the creative faculties, increase the capacity for enjoyment and develop a spirit of critical appreciation of arts, literature and other creative activities.

The long range goal of educational planning is then to

94 National Education Policy (NEP), 2020 and the Role of Teachers

make available diverse networks of facilities and programmes for education, combining formal and non-formal modes of learning. It should enable all citizens to acquire literacy, numeracy, computational skills, basic understanding of the surrounding world and functional skills of relevance to daily life and to local environment.

The intensity of the problems of education and population growth in rural areas corresponds to the educational deprivation of women. The broad priorities, therefore, should prepare the ground for the spread of literacy and primary education through socio-economic justice and to remove the traditional constraints on the status and education of rural women, in particular. A demand for education, modernization and efficiency has to be stimulated through a general awakening and mobilisation of the rural communities especially in the educationally backward states.

The fulfilment of these objectives would lead to the development of an integrated personality in the individual, which should be the first and foremost aim of any system of education.

7.6 Education and Women Empowerment

There is an increased awareness that education is one of the most valuable means of achieving gender equality and the empowerment of women. Education is seen as a critical factor in breaking the inter-generational cycle of transmission of poverty. The power of education lies not just in imparting formal literacy, but rather in the acquisition of skills that enable access to multiple literacy—economic, legal, health, political and media etc.

Education is a key intervention in initiating and sustaining processes of empowerment. Good quality education can help women and marginalized communities to: (a) improve their status, (b) enable them to have greater access to information and resources and (c) challenge various forms of discrimination. Education helps strengthen democratic processes as it allows for greater and more equitable participation. Being educated, leads to

Education, Women Empowerment and Literacy Rates   95

greater self-confidence and self-esteem. It enables engagement with development processes and institutions of governance from a position of strength. Poor women from socially disadvantaged communities are invariably not literate and therefore find themselves at a disadvantage when participating in development processes.

It is, however, important to recognise that while being literate or educated is necessary for empowerment, it does not automatically ensure it. For that a society needs an education system which is of good quality and promotes critical thinking. From the perspective of gender this means that education and literacy should enable women and girls to critically analyse their situations, raise questions about their subordination and help them make informed choices. It is well-known that the institution of schooling is an important site for socialisation that actually reinforces rather than challenges patriarchy and gender discrimination. It is in this context that the content and pedagogy of education become critical considerations.

The focus of educational planning is generally on formal education but this is only one dimension of the educational provisioning, especially when needs of deprived women are under consideration and empowerment of women is the main objective. Though the content of education and classroom pedagogy are critical to altering gender and other social relations it has not been paid the attention it deserves. Efforts to make curricula gender-sensitive have been undertaken but can be considered initial attempts as they have remained largely at the level of removing stereotypes or increasing visibility and have not looked at gender in terms of social relations.

Problems related to the representation of marginalized communities continue to exist and contribute to the deep sense of alienation of these communities from the mainstream education system and a reason for children dropping out. Sexuality is addressed in a problematic manner in educational materials. It is either related to population or reproductive health or seen as a

96 National Education Policy (NEP), 2020 and the Role of Teachers

problem associated with promiscuity and shame. Classrooms need to be transformed into spaces that can help girls think critically. Discriminatory practices based on identity-based prejudices need to be monitored and stopped. Corporal punishment, which is wide spread, needs to be checked. The role of the teacher is naturally crucial in this context.

Women, though they make half the world's population, constitute the largest group which is excluded from the benefits of development. Work participation rate of women is much less than that of men. The multiple roles of women and the meagre ability to access resources and available assets are areas of concern. It is important to emphasise that women require adequate security and protection to be self-reliant.

Special attention has to be paid to women workers because of problems peculiar to them. Comparatively speaking, they are much less organised. They also suffer from certain social prejudices and physical disabilities.

7.6.1 Adverse Effects of Globalization on Women: With the growing globalization and liberalization of the economy as well as increased privatization of services, women as a whole have been left behind and not been able to partake of the fruits of success. Mainstreaming of women into the new and emerging areas of growth is imperative. This will require training and skill upgradation in emerging trades, encouraging more women to take up vocational training and employment in the boom sectors. This will also require women to migrate to cities and metros for work. Provision of safe housing, and other gender friendly facilities at work will need to be provided.

Another facet of globalization is related to the fact that many persons especially women will be severely affected with the advent of setting up of industrial parks, national highways, special economic zones (SEZs) etc. as huge tracts of farm land are likely to be acquired for this purpose. This would require massive resettlement of the displaced persons and their families. It is therefore essential that a viable resettlement

Education, Women Empowerment and Literacy Rates 97

policy and strategy is formulated and put in place immediately which clearly reflects the needs of women impacted by globalization/displacement.

With the removal of all quantitative restrictions on the import of various products, the self-employed women's groups, especially in the informal sector, have started facing competition from the low-priced imported consumer goods which are invading the Indian market. Although this has the imminent danger of displacing a large number of employed/self-employed women, but at the same time, the process of globalization has also opened up opportunities for women entrepreneurs for exporting their products to the markets all over the world. Globalization has thus opened up new challenges for the realization of the goal of women's empowerment. Hence, strategies should be designed to enhance the capacity of women and empower them to cope with the negative economic and social impacts of the globalization process.

Several studies have indicated that adverse consequences of globalisation are disproportionately borne by women. Increased mechanization leading to displacement of female unskilled workers, increased migration of male workers in traditionally women-dominated areas, increase in female-headed household due to migration of males are some of the trends established in various studies.

Globalization has presented new challenges for the realization of the goal of women's equality, the gender impact of which has not been systematically evaluated fully. However, it is evident that there is a need for re-framing policies for access to employment and equality of employment. Benefits of the growing global economy have been unevenly distributed leading to wider economic disparities, the feminization of poverty, increased gender inequality through deteriorating working conditions and unsafe working environment especially in the informal economy and rural areas. Strategies need to be designed to enhance the capacity of women and empower them to meet the negative social and economic impacts, which may flow from the globalization process.

With upgradation of skills, opportunities for employment of women exist in several areas such as health services, food processing and crafts. Key areas of concern include women in small subsistence farming households, women workers in garment and textiles who will face increased competition after the phasing out of the Multi Fibre Agreement in 2005, and women displaced by new technologies in sectors such as construction, which have traditionally absorbed large numbers of women.

With the onset of trade liberalisation, women in India today are linked to the global economy to a very significant extent, as producers, entrepreneurs, service providers, consumers and citizens. There is a need to identify capacity constraints and entry barriers that prevent women from securing gains from trade. Trade-related awareness and capacity building of the women stakeholders need to be prioritised.

The globalization process has, in some countries, resulted in policy shifts in favour of more open trade and financial flows, privatization of state-owned enterprises and in many cases lower public spending particularly on social services. This change has transformed patterns of production and accelerated technological advances in information and communication and affected the lives of women, both as workers and consumers. In a large number of countries, particularly in developing and least developed countries, these changes have also adversely impacted on the lives of women and have increased inequality. The gender impact of these changes has not been systematically evaluated. Globalization has also affected cultural values, lifestyles and forms of communication.

In countries with economies in transition women are bearing most of the hardships induced by the economic restructuring and being the first to lose jobs in times of

Education, Women Empowerment and Literacy Rates   99

recession. They are being squeezed out from fast growth sectors. Loss of childcare facilities due to elimination or privatization of state work places, increased need for older care without the corresponding facilities, continuing inequality of access to training for finding re-employment and to productive assets for entering or expanding businesses are current challenges facing women in these countries.

7.7 Women in Decision-making

There has been growing acceptance of the importance to society of the full participation of women in decision-making and power at all levels and in all fora, including inter-governmental, governmental, and non-governmental sectors. In some countries, women have also attained higher positions in these spheres. An increasing number of countries applied affirmative and positive action policies, including quota systems or voluntary agreements in some countries, measurable goals and targets, developed training programmes for women's leadership and introduced measures to reconcile family and work responsibilities of both women and men. National mechanisms and machineries for the advancement of women as well as national and international networks of women politicians, parliamentarians, activists and professionals in various fields have been established or upgraded and strengthened.

Despite general acceptance of the need for a gender balance in decision-making bodies at all levels, a gap between *de jure* and *de facto* equality has persisted. Notwithstanding substantial improvements of *de jure* equality between women and men, the actual participation of women at the highest levels of national and international decision-making has not significantly changed and gross under-representation of women in decision-making bodies in all areas, including *inter alia* politics, conflict prevention and resolution mechanisms, the economy, the environment and the media hinders the inclusion of a gender perspective in these critical spheres of influence. Women continue to be underrepresented at the

100 National Education Policy (NEP), 2020 and the Role of Teachers

legislative, ministerial and sub-ministerial levels, as well as at the highest levels of the corporate sector and other social and economic institutions. Traditionally assigned gender roles limit women's choices in education and careers and compel women to assume the burden for household responsibilities.

7.8 Trends in Literacy Rates

Though the level and quality of education can be measured in a number of ways, literacy figures are essential in any measurement of educational attainment. The level of literacy is an important and the most basic index of the educational achievements of an economy.

Besides overall education, female education has a special role in the development process; therefore, we also take a separate look at female literacy as an important determinant of development.

Literacy levels in a country are a measure of its degree of commitment to social justice. A literate environment is essential for ensuring universal elementary education, reducing child mortality, curbing population growth, ensuring gender equality and acquiring essential livelihood skills.

Over the decades, literacy rates in India have shown a substantial improvement. The total literacy rate which was only 18.33 percent in 1951, rose to 52.21 percent in 1991, and further to 65.4 percent in 2001 and subsequently increased to 74.04 percent in 2011. According to the Census of India, 2011, the literacy rate has gone up to 82.14 percent for males and 65.46 percent for females. Female literacy rate has shown much higher growth, increasing by 11.30 percentage points as against 6.29 for males thus reducing the male-female differential in literacy rates from 21.7 in 2001 to 16.68 in 2011 (Table 7.1).

Literacy rates in India have risen sharply from 18.3 percent in 1951 to 74.04 percent in 2011. Nevertheless, India continues to lag behind several other developing countries in the region such as China (86 percent) and Sri Lanka (92 percent).

To enlist the support of all concerned and to mobilize extra budgetary resources for the education sector, *Bharat Shiksha Kosh*, a registered society has been set up for receiving contributions, donations or endowments from individuals, Central and State governments, and non-resident Indians (NRIs) for various educational purposes. Emphasizing the role of education, Eleventh Five Year Plan (2007-12) observed, "The role of education in facilitating social and economic progress is well recognized. It opens up opportunities leading to both individual and group entitlements. Education in its broadest sense of development of youth is the most crucial input for empowering people with skills and knowledge and giving them access to productive employment in future. Improvements in education are not only expected to enhance efficiency but also augment the overall quality of life". [5]

Table 7.1: Literacy Rates in India (1951-2011)

(percent)

Census Year	Persons	Males	Females	Male-Female Gap in Literacy Rate
1951	18.33	27.16	8.66	18.30
1961	28.30	40.40	15.35	25.05
1971	34.45	45.96	21.97	23.98
1981	43.57	56.38	29.76	26.62
1991	52.21	64.13	39.29	24.84
2001	65.38	75.85	54.16	21.70
2011	74.04	82.14	65.46	16.68

Source: Census of India.

7.9 Promotion of Indian Languages, Arts, and Culture

According to NEP, 2020, "India is a treasure trove of culture, developed over thousands of years and manifested in the form of arts, works of literature, customs, traditions, linguistic expressions, artefacts, heritage sites, and more. Crores of people from around the world partake in, enjoy, and benefit from this cultural wealth daily, in the form of visiting India for tourism, experiencing Indian hospitality, purchasing India's handicrafts and handmade textiles, reading the classical

102 National Education Policy (NEP), 2020 and the Role of Teachers

literature of India, practicing yoga and meditation, being inspired by Indian philosophy, participating in India's unique festivals, appreciating India's diverse music and art, and watching Indian films, amongst many other aspects. It is this cultural and natural wealth that truly makes India, "Incredible India", as per India's tourism slogan. The preservation and promotion of India's cultural wealth must be considered a high priority for the country, as it is truly important for the nation's identity as well as for its economy.

The promotion of Indian arts and culture is important not only for the nation but also for the individual. Cultural awareness and expression are among the major competencies considered important to develop in children, in order to provide them with a sense of identity, belonging, as well as an appreciation of other cultures and identities. It is through the development of a strong sense and knowledge of their own cultural history, arts, languages, and traditions that children can build a positive cultural identity and self-esteem. Thus, cultural awareness and expression are important contributors both to individual as well as societal well-being.

The arts form a major medium for imparting culture. The arts, besides strengthening cultural identity, awareness, and uplifting societies, are well known to enhance cognitive and creative abilities in individuals and increase individual happiness. The happiness/well-being, cognitive development, and cultural identity of individuals are important reasons that Indian arts of all kinds must be offered to students at all levels of education, starting with early childhood care and education.

Language, of course, is inextricably linked to art and culture. Different languages 'see' the world differently, and the structure of a language, therefore, determines a native speaker's perception of experience. In particular, languages influence the way people of a given culture speak with others, including with family members, authority figures, peers, and strangers, and influence the tone of conversation. The tone, perception of experience, and familiarity/*apnapan* inherent in

Education, Women Empowerment and Literacy Rates 103

conversations among speakers of a common language are a reflection and record of a culture. Culture is, thus, encased in our languages. Art, in the form of literature, plays, music, film, etc. cannot be fully appreciated without language. In order to preserve and promote culture, one must preserve and promote a culture's languages". [6]

7.10 Recruitment and Deployment of Teachers

The teacher must be at the centre of the fundamental reforms in the education system. The new education policy must help re-establish teachers, at all levels, as the most respected and essential members of our society, because they truly shape our next generation of citizens. It must do everything to empower teachers and help them to do their job as effectively as possible. The new education policy must help recruit the very best and brightest to enter the teaching profession at all levels, by ensuring livelihood, respect, dignity, and autonomy, while also instilling in the system basic methods of quality control and accountability.

Teachers truly shape the future of our children and, therefore, the future of our nation. It is because of this noblest role that the teacher in India was the most respected member of society. Only the very best and most learned became teachers. Society gave teachers, or gurus, what they needed to pass on their knowledge, skills, and ethics optimally to students. The quality of teacher education, recruitment, deployment, service conditions, and empowerment of teachers is not where it should be, and consequently the quality and motivation of teachers does not reach the desired standards. The high respect for teachers and the high status of the teaching profession must be restored so as to inspire the best to enter the teaching profession. The motivation and empowerment of teachers is required to ensure the best possible future for our children and our nation.

Teacher education is vital in creating a pool of schoolteachers that will shape the next generation. Teacher preparation is an activity that requires multidisciplinary perspectives and knowledge, formation of dispositions and values, and development of practice under the best mentors. Teachers must be grounded in Indian values, languages, knowledge, ethos, and traditions including tribal traditions, while also being well-versed in the latest advances in education and pedagogy.

As regards the recruitment and deployment of teachers, the National Education Policy (NEP), 2020 states, "To ensure that outstanding students enter the teaching profession—especially from rural areas—a large number of merit-based scholarships shall be instituted across the country for studying quality 4-year integrated B.Ed. programmes. In rural areas, special merit-based scholarships will be established that also include preferential employment in their local areas upon successful completion of their B.Ed. programmes. Such scholarships will provide local job opportunities to local students, especially female students, so that these students serve as local-area role models and as highly qualified teachers who speak the local language. Incentives will be provided for teachers to take up teaching jobs in rural areas, especially in areas that are currently facing acute shortage of quality teachers. A key incentive for teaching in rural schools will be the provision of local housing near or on the school premises or increased housing allowances.

The harmful practice of excessive teacher transfers will be halted, so that students have continuity in their role models and educational environments. Transfers will occur in very special circumstances, as suitably laid down in a structured manner by State/UT governments. Furthermore, transfers will be conducted through an online computerized system that ensures transparency.

Teacher eligibility tests (TETs) will be strengthened to inculcate better test material, both in terms of content and pedagogy. The TETs will also be extended to cover teachers across all stages (foundational, preparatory, middle and secondary) of school education. For subject teachers, suitable

Education, Women Empowerment and Literacy Rates 105

TET or NTA test scores in the corresponding subjects will also be taken into account for recruitment. To gauge passion and motivation for teaching, a classroom demonstration or interview will become an integral part of teacher hiring at schools and school complexes. These interviews would also be used to assess comfort and proficiency in teaching in the local language, so that every school/school complex has at least some teachers who can converse with students in the local language and other prevalent home languages of students. Teachers in private schools also must have qualified similarly through TET, a demonstration/interview, and knowledge of local language(s).

To ensure an adequate number of teachers across subjects—particularly in subjects such as art, physical education, vocational education, and languages—teachers could be recruited to a school or school complex and the sharing of teachers across schools could be considered in accordance with the grouping-of-schools adopted by State/UT governments". [7]

Endnotes
1. Government of India, Ministry of Human Resource Development, *National Education Policy 2020*, p. 3.
2. Government of India, Planning Commission, *Twelfth Five Year Plan (2012-17)*, Volume III, para 21.1.
3. *National Education Policy 2020*, op. cit., p. 4.
4. Ibid., p. 36.
5. Government of India, Planning Commission, *Eleventh Five Year Plan (2007-12)*, Volume II, p. 1.
6. *National Education Policy 2020*, op. cit., 53.
7. Ibid., p. 20.

8

Elementary Education

From the stand point of priorities within the field of education, importance should be attached, in terms of coverage, to children in the school going age-groups and those among the socially under-privileged groups. This early childhood stage is the period of maximum learning and intellectual development of the child and hence of great potential educational significance.

8.1 Elementary Education Policy

The provision of free and compulsory primary education is the first necessary step towards establishing equality of opportunity for every citizen. The foremost task in the field of basic education is the improvement of technique and the development of methods, by which it can be passed on to the vast majority of teachers of rather low educational qualifications and average ability.

Elementary education comprising primary (Class I-V) and upper primary (Class VI-VIII) forms the foundation of the education pyramid. Unless this foundation is strengthened, it will not be feasible to achieve the goal of universal access to *quality education* for all. A major achievement in recent years has been the establishment of Constitutional and legal underpinnings for achieving universal elementary education. The Right of Children to Free and Compulsory Education (RTE) Act, 2009, became operative on April 1, 2010.

In India, within the education sector, elementary education has been given the highest priority in terms of sub-sectoral allocations and the number of schemes launched by the Central Government to meet the needs of the educationally disadvantaged. Elementary education, i.e. classes I-VIII

Elementary Education

consisting of primary (I-V) and upper primary (VI-VIII) is the foundation of the structure of the education system.

8.1.1 National Policy on Education (NPE), 1986: NPE, as modified in 1992, emphasized the following three aspects in relation to elementary education:

1. Universal access and enrolment.
2. Universal retention of children up to 14 years of age.
3. Substantial improvement in the quality of education to enable all children to achieve essential levels of learning.

NPE emphasised that education must play a positive and interventionist role in correcting social and regional imbalance, empowering women, and in securing a rightful place for the disadvantaged and the minorities. Government is firmly committed to providing education for all, the priority areas being free and compulsory elementary education, covering children with special needs, eradication of illiteracy, education for women's equality, and special focus on the education of scheduled castes (SCs), scheduled tribes (STs) and minorities.

8.1.2 Twelfth Five Year Plan (2012-17) on Elementary Education: According to Twelfth Plan, "The overarching goal of the Twelfth Plan is to enrol out of school children (OoSC), reduce dropouts and improve learning outcomes across the elementary school years. In order to enrol OoSC, strengthening of institutional capacity, developing an appropriate statistical base, harmonising the definition of OoSC and finally identification and mainstreaming of all children into age-appropriate class would be needed. Reduction in dropout rates is closely linked to quality. There is a need for a system-wide effort to move the focus of all activity in elementary education from schooling to learning. This entails a shift at every level, macro and micro, whether in planning, resource allocation and implementation or measurement of processes and practices that is designed to achieve significant, substantial and continuous improvement in children's learning outcomes. The entire process of education should be firmly anchored to the notion that every child must be in school and learning well. [1]

8.1.3 National Education Policy (NEP), 2020 on Elementary Education:
NEP, 2020 states, "One of the primary goals of the schooling system must be to ensure that children are enrolled in and are attending school. Through initiatives such as the Sarva Shiksha Abhiyan (now the Samagra Shiksha) and the Right to Education Act, India has made remarkable strides in recent years in attaining near-universal enrolment in elementary education". [2]

8.2 Select Programmes for Elementary Education: These are as under:

8.2.1 *Sarva Shiksha Abhiyan* (SSA):
Launched in November 2000, SSA (now called Samagra Shiksha) is a comprehensive programme and the main vehicle for providing elementary education to all children. The goals of SSA are the following.

1. All children in school, education guarantee centre, alternate school, back-to-school camp by 2005.
2. Bridge all gender and social category gaps at the primary stage by 2007 and at elementary education level by 2010.
3. Universal retention by 2010.
4. Focus on elementary education of satisfactory quality with emphasis on education for life.

SSA aims at universalizing access to education at primary and upper primary levels through new schools, additional classrooms, teachers, special training for out-of-school children, provisions for textbooks, uniforms, residential facilities, transportation, training, etc.

SSA, implemented in partnership with the States, addresses the needs of 192 million children in the age group of 6-14 years. It covers 9.72 lakh existing primary and upper primary schools and 36.95 lakh teachers.

SSA is the culmination of all previous endeavours and experiences in implementing various education programmes. SSA has been the single largest holistic programme addressing all aspects of elementary education. SSA has brought primary

Elementary Education

education to the doorstep of millions of children and enrolled them, including first generation learners, through successive fast track initiatives in hitherto unserved and underserved habitations.

Strong efforts are needed to address the systemic issues of regular functioning of schools, teacher attendance and competence, accountability of educational administrators, pragmatic teacher transfer and promotion policies, effective decentralization of school management and transfer of powers to panchayati raj institutions (PRIs), to build upon the gains of SSA.

8.2.2 *Kasturba Gandhi Balika Vidyalaya Scheme* (KGBVS): KGBVS was launched in July 2004 to set up 750 residential schools at elementary level for girls belonging predominantly to the scheduled castes, scheduled tribes, other backward classes and minorities in educationally backward blocks (EBBs). All 750 KGBVs have now been sanctioned by the Government of India, with 117 KGBVs (15.6 percent) allocated to blocks with substantial minority population. A minimum of 75 percent of the enrolment in KGBVs is reserved for girls from the target groups and the remaining 25 percent is open for girls belonging to the below poverty line (BPL) category.

8.2.3 District Primary Education Programme (DPEP): Started in 1994, DPEP, an externally aided project, aimed at the holistic development of primary education covering Classes I to V. It had specific objectives of reducing the dropout rate to less than 10 percent, reducing disparities among gender and social groups in the enrolment to less than 5 percent and improving the level of learning achievement compared to the baseline surveys. However, these ambitious targets could not be achieved. Still, DPEP brought about a sea change in the implementation of school education programme with its decentralized approach and focus on community participation. At its peak, DPEP covered 273 districts in 17 States.

8.2.4 National Programme of Nutritional Support to Primary Education (NP-NSPE): NP-NSPE, popularly known as Mid-day Meal Scheme (MDMS), was launched on

110   National Education Policy (NEP), 2020 and the Role of Teachers

August 15, 1995 with the objective to boost the universalisation of primary education by impacting upon enrolment, attendance, retention and nutritional needs of children studying in class I-V.

The Scheme aims at providing hot cooked mid-day meals to all children attending elementary classes in government, local body, government-aided and national child labour project schools, as well as centres under the Education Guarantee Scheme (EGS) and alternate and innovative education centres, including madrasas/maqtabs. Social audit has been introduced to monitor the scheme, including testing of food samples by accredited labs. The scheme is being monitored by the MDM-MIS web portal which has scope for integrating with the interactive voice response system (IVRS) for real-time monitoring through community participation.

NP-NSPE is the world's largest school feeding programme involving preparation of a hot meal everyday. It provides free foodgrains, cooking cost, transport subsidy and other facilities. The scheme was revised and universalised in September 2004 and central assistance was provided @ ₹ 1 per child/per school day for converting foodgrains into hot cooked meals for children in classes IV in Government, Local Body and Government-aided schools, and Education Guarantee Scheme (EGS) and Alternate and Innovative Education (AIE) centres. The maximum permissible transport subsidy was revised for Special Category States from ₹ 50 to ₹ 100 per quintal and for other States to ₹ 75 per quintal.

The scheme was further revised in June 2006 to enhance the minimum cooking cost to ₹ 2.00 per child/per school day to provide 450 calories and 12 grams of protein. The revised scheme also provided assistance for construction of kitchen-cum-stores @ ₹ 60,000 per unit in a phased manner in primary schools and procurement of kitchen devices (utensils etc) @ ₹ 5,000 per school. From the year 2009 onwards, changes in food norms have been revised to ensure balanced and nutritious diet to children of upper primary group by

Elementary Education   111

increasing the quantity of pulses from 25 to 30 grams, vegetables from 65 to 75 grams and by decreasing the quantity of oil and fat from 10 grams to 7.5 grams. During 2012-13, 10.68 crore children (elementary level) were covered in 12.12 lakh schools. 10.45 crore children were covered in 11.58 lakh schools during 2013-14.

8.2.5 *Pradhan Mantri Gramodaya Yojana* **(PMGY):** This programme was launched during 2000-01 and envisages Additional Central Assistance (ACA) for basic minimum services in certain priority areas. The scheme has six components covering elementary education, primary health, rural shelter, rural drinking water, nutrition and rural electrification. A minimum of 10 percent of ACA for all components except nutrition (for which it is 15 percent) has been fixed. The allocation for the remaining 35 percent of ACA would be decided by the States and UTs among the components of the scheme, as per their priorities. Funds for elementary education sector under PMGY are utilized to further the goal of universalisation of elementary education.

8.2.6 National Programme for Education of Girls at Elementary Level (NPEGEL): It is an important component of SSA. Launched in July 2003, NPEGEL provides additional support by way of girl-child friendly schools, stationery, uniforms etc. for girls' education in educationally backward blocks (EBB), and in other areas for elementary education of under privileged and disadvantaged sections. EBBs are blocks with female literacy below, and gender gap above, the national average. Apart from EBBs, NPEGEL is also implemented in blocks of districts which are not covered under EBBs but have at least 5 percent SC/ST population and where SC/ST female literacy is below 10 percent, and also in select urban slums. In the Tenth Five Year Plan, an amount of ₹ 1064.80 crore was earmarked for this programme.

NPEGEL provides for development of a model school in every cluster with more intense community mobilisation and supervision of girls' enrolment in schools. Gender-sensitisation of teachers, development of gender-sensitive learning materials and

112   National Education Policy (NEP), 2020 and the Role of Teachers

provision of need-based incentives like stationery, workbooks and uniforms are some of the objectives under NPEGEL. It is being implemented in about 3,164 educationally backward blocks in 25 States.

8.2.7 Education Guarantee Scheme and Alternative and Innovative Education (EGS&AIE): Another important component of SSA is the EGS&AIE. It is specially designed to provide access to elementary education to children in school-less habitations and out-of-school children. It supports flexible strategies for out-of-school children through bridge courses, residential camps, drop-in centres, summer camps, remedial coaching etc.

8.2.8 *Mahila Samakhya* (MS): MS, an externally aided project for women's empowerment, was started with Dutch assistance in 1989. Since 2005-06 it is being funded by Government of India. The programme endeavours to create an environment for women to learn at their own pace, set their own priorities and seek knowledge and information to make informed choices. It has strengthened women's abilities to effectively participate in village level education programmes. The programme is being implemented in 9 States covering 83 districts. Madhya Pradesh and Chhattisgarh have registered MS societies through which the programme is initiated. MS provides for vocational and skill development as well as educational development of adolescent girls and women in rural areas.

8.2.9 *Prarambhik Shiksha Kosh* (PSK): PSK was constituted on November 14, 2005 to receive the proceeds of the education cess imposed through Finance (No. 2) Act, 2004. PSK is a separate, dedicated, non-lapsable fund to be maintained by the Ministry of Human Resource Development.

8.3 Problem Areas in Elementary Education

In education, the elementary sector is besieged by numerous systemic problems such as inadequate school infrastructure, presence of single-teacher schools, high teacher absenteeism (especially in rural areas), large-scale teacher

Elementary Education 113

vacancies, inadequate equipment etc. This brings into focus the role of decentralization and people's participation in the provision of basic services. It is essential that control over schools and teachers should be transferred to local bodies, having a direct interest in teacher performance.

In view of the shortage of funds, Government can accept only limited responsibility in this field, confined to research in evolving methods suited to needs, training of teachers, helping private agencies who take up this work in the rural areas by grants-in-aid and running a few model *balwadis* or nursery schools in each State. In labour areas, it should be the responsibility of industry to make provision for such schools. In other areas, the major burden of organising and running *balwadis* should be borne by local bodies. Where resources do not allow the opening of fulltime institutions, day nurseries, working for a few hours in mornings and evenings, should be organised by voluntary workers.

The quality of teaching in elementary schools is also not what it should be. Teacher absenteeism is widespread, teachers are not adequately trained and the quality of pedagogy is poor. These deficiencies need to be corrected to improve the quality of education at the elementary level, especially in rural areas. Addressing the quality issue in schools is critical for the effective development of human capabilities and for achieving the objective of equality of opportunities. The quality of teachers and, even more important, their motivation and accountability, needs to be improved. Many of the children who are presently in school are first-generation learners, and these children need supplementary instruction. This is not easy due to shortage of qualified teachers in many schools across the country.

Endnotes

1. Government of India, Planning Commission, *Twelfth Five Year Plan (2012-17)*, Volume III, Chapter 21.
2. Government of India, Ministry of Human Resource Development, *National Education Policy 2020*, p. 10.

9

Secondary and Vocational Education

9.1 Secondary Education

A sound system of secondary education, which offers openings in a large number of different directions, is an essential foundation for economic development on modern lines. With the expansion of elementary education, an increasing number of students reach the secondary stage. The year 2008-09 was a momentous year for secondary education in India when a new Centrally-sponsored scheme to universalise education at secondary stage was launched.

9.1.1 Requirements of a Sound Secondary Education System: In the first place, secondary education must be closely related to the psychological needs of the adolescents for whom it is being designed.

Secondly, it should be vitally related to the existing socio-economic situation, to the directive principles of State policy laid down in the Constitution and the approved schemes for social and economic reconstruction. In order to equip the youth adequately for the needs of the existing socio-economic situation, it is necessary to give secondary education a vocational bias. At present this education is mainly academic and does not provide sufficient scope for adolescents with varying aptitudes especially those with a marked practical bent of mind.

Thirdly, secondary education should grow from the education that is being given at the primary stage, i.e. it should be closely integrated with the basic education and its essential underlying principles. There should be no wide variation in the method of teaching and curriculum of the basic and the secondary school. The planning of the secondary education must also have in view the creation of leadership in the

Secondary and Vocational Education

intermediate level, because for the majority of students, formal education comes to an end at this stage.

To this end, suitable types of multilateral or unilateral schools offering parallel courses should be provided and the personnel for vocational guidance should be trained. The standards to be attained should be high enough, on the one hand to make the majority of students whose education ends at the secondary stage to be efficient workers and, on the other, to enable the minority who proceed to higher education to profit from the instructions they receive at these institutions. In view of the role it has to play between the basic and the higher stage, the planning of secondary education requires considerable care and attention.

9.1.2 Increase in the Demand for Secondary Education: Development of the economy and the large increase in the number of secondary schools and in the number of students of the age-group 14-17 enrolled in them have altered the character of the demands which secondary education is called upon to meet. New social groups are seeking education and are coming within its influence. Expansion has brought into secondary schools a larger range of abilities and aptitudes. Secondary schools have to be so reorganised that they provide diversified educational service to pupils according to their needs. In the middle and lower grades of many branches of economic life, in administration, rural development, commerce, industry and the professions, the requirements of trained manpower have to be met after the necessary training, by products of secondary schools.

Secondary school teachers have to be thoroughly prepared for handling the new subjects efficiently. The teacher education programme at the pre-service level has also to be reorganised in line with the changes that have taken place at the secondary level. The standard of science education has to be raised to a level which will effectively support the future scientific advance of the nation. Shortcomings which have been observed in the working of the multi-purpose schools have to be remedied and the scheme placed on a stable footing.

Educational and vocational guidance programmes have to be extended to reach as many schools and pupils as possible. Measures should be taken to strengthen the entire programme of the secondary school reorganisation, such as improvement in craft teaching, organisation of school libraries, the better use of audio-visual techniques

With a dramatic growth in elementary education enrolments and improvements in retention and transition rates in recent years, particularly amongst the more disadvantaged groups, there is an increasing pressure on the secondary schools to admit more students. With the enforcement of RTE Act and further improvement in retention and transition rates, demand for secondary schooling will grow rapidly in the coming years. Meeting this demand is critical for three reasons.

First, the secondary education fulfils large manpower needs of the semi- organized and the organised sectors of the economy. Second, it is the supply chain for higher education. And, finally, it caters to the needs of teachers for primary schooling. Low participation rates and poor quality at the secondary stage are a bottleneck in improving both the higher education participation and the schooling at the elementary stage.

Further, there are both social and economic benefits of secondary schooling. While there are clear improvements in health, gender equality and living conditions with secondary education, investments in secondary schooling have high marginal rates of return. Thus, the country needs to move towards universalisation of opportunity to attend secondary schooling of adequate quality. With enrolment in elementary education reaching near universal levels, there would be an opportunity to move towards universal access to secondary education.

Secondary education sector prepares students in the age group of 14-18 years for entry into higher education as well as for the world of work. The success of *Sarva Shiksha Abhiyan* (SSA) in achieving large-scale enrolment of children in regular and alternate schools has thrown open the challenge of

Secondary and Vocational Education 117

expanding access to secondary education. Rapid changes in technology and the demand for skills also make it necessary that young people acquire more than eight years of elementary education to acquire the necessary skills to compete successfully in the labour market. Moreover, secondary education serves as a bridge between elementary and higher education.

9.1.3 Secondary Education Commission, 1953: Problems of secondary education were reviewed by the Secondary Education Commission whose report was presented in 1953. The Commission considered the basic shortcomings of the existing secondary schools and observed that the curricula being followed and the traditional methods of teaching did not give students sufficient insight into the every day world in which they lived and failed to train the whole personality of the pupil. In the past excessive emphasis on the study of the English language led to neglect of many other subjects. With the increase in the size of classes the personal contact of teachers and students diminished and discipline and character were not sufficiently inculcated. While piecemeal reforms were introduced from time to time, there was need for new re-orientation in the system of secondary education as a whole. The Commission, therefore, made proposals for bringing about a greater diversity and comprehensiveness in educational courses and providing more comprehensive courses which would include both general and vocational subjects. It did not contemplate any artificial division between *general or cultural* education and *practical* or *vocational* or *technical* education.

In the new organisational pattern, which the Commission recommended, it was visualised that following the 4 or 5 year period of primary or junior basic education, there would be a middle or senior basic or junior secondary stage of 3 years and a higher secondary stage of 4 years. The first degree course would then be of 3 years duration. The Commission recommended the establishment of: (a) multi-purpose schools, (b) technical schools either separately or as part of multi-purpose schools and (c) special facilities for agricultural education in rural schools. The provision in all secondary schools for courses in languages, general science, social studies and a craft as a common core was also proposed for general adoption. These recommendations formed the basis of programmes adopted by the Centre and the States in the Second Five Year Plan (1956-61).

9.1.4 Centrally Managed Schools: The Central Government is managing and fully funding four types of schools, viz.

1. Kendriya Vidyalayas (KVs).
2. Navodaya Vidyalayas (NVs).
3. Central Tibetan Schools (CTSs).
4. National Institute of Open Schooling (NIOS).

KVs cater to the educational needs of the wards of transferable Central Government and public sector employees. NVs are pace setting residential co-educational schools providing quality education to talented children predominantly from rural areas. There are 71 CTSs with a total enrolment of 10,000 children. NIOS provides opportunities for continuing education to those who missed completing school education. NIOS Centres have also been set up in UAE, Kuwait, Nepal, Muscat and Qatar.

Central Government also supports autonomous organisations like National Council of Educational Research and Training (NCERT) and Central Board of Secondary Education (CBSE).

The thrust of secondary education is on improving access and reducing disparities by emphasising the Common School System in which it is mandatory for schools in a particular area to take students from low income families in the neighbourhood. Revision of curricula has taken place with emphasis on vocationalisation and employment-oriented courses, expansion and diversification of the open learning system, reorganization of teacher training and greater use of information and communication technologies.

9.1.5 Rashtriya Madhyamik Shiksha Abhiyan (RMSA):

Although there is considerable focus on providing secondary school access, the dropout rates between elementary and secondary schools continue to be high, and between the secondary and post-secondary stage they are even higher. This is a particularly serious problem for girls, who have to travel longer distances to attend secondary schools. Curricular and examination reforms in secondary schooling should receive special attention aimed at fostering critical thinking and analytical skills, and preparing students for further education. All this requires innovative approaches, some of which are already in evidence in certain States.

RMSA was launched in March 2009 with the objective of enhancing access to secondary education and improving its quality. The implementation of the scheme started from 2009-10. It envisaged raising the enrolment rate at secondary stage from 52.26 percent in 2005-06 to 75 percent within five years by providing a secondary school within reasonable distance of any habitation. The other objectives included improving quality of education imparted at secondary level by ensuring that all secondary schools conform to prescribed norms, removing gender, socio-economic and disability barriers, providing universal access to secondary-level education by 2017.

The major objectives of the RMSA are as under:

1. To raise the minimum level of education to class X and universalise access to secondary education.
2. To ensure good-quality secondary education with focus on Science, Mathematics and English.
3. To reduce the gender, social and regional gaps in enrolments, dropouts and improving retention.

The interventions supported under RMSA include the following:

1. Upgrading of upper primary schools to secondary schools.
2. Strengthening of existing secondary schools.
3. Providing additional classrooms, science laboratories, libraries, computer rooms, art, craft and culture rooms,

120 National Education Policy (NEP), 2020 and the Role of Teachers

toilet blocks and water facilities in schools.
4. Providing in-service training of teachers.
5. Providing for major repairs of school buildings and residential quarters for teachers.

9.1.6 Inclusive Education for the Disabled at Secondary Stage (IEDSS): IEDSS scheme was launched in 2009-10 replacing the earlier scheme of integrated education for disabled children (IEDC). It provides 100 percent Central assistance for inclusive education of disabled children studying in Classes IX-XII in government, local body, and government-aided schools. The aim of the scheme is to facilitate continuation of education of children with special needs up to higher secondary level. The scheme provides for personal requirements of the children in the form of assistive devices, helpers, transport, hostel, learning material, scholarship for the girl child etc. up to ₹ 3,000 per disabled child per annum.

Apart from RMSA and IEDSS, as explained above, there are several other Centrally-sponsored schemes that benefit secondary school students of different categories and background. These are as under:
1. Model Schools Scheme.
2. Girls Hostel Scheme.
3. Scheme of Vocational Education.
4. National Means-cum Merit Scholarship Scheme.
5. National Incentive to Girls.
6. Appointment of Language Teachers.

9.1.7 Policy Requirements for Secondary Education: Secondary and higher secondary education are important terminal stages in the system of general education and provide a first stage for linking education with the world of work. It is at this point that options are exercised by the youth to enter the world of employment or to go for technical training or to pursue higher education. With the expansion of the base of education at the elementary stage, increasing number of students, including a large number of first generation learners, reach secondary education. Facilities have to be provided for

Secondary and Vocational Education 121

their education since such education is the only means of social mobility and economic independence, particularly among the socially disadvantaged. Care has to be taken to ensure that secondary education also prepares them for a long-term career as part of the stock of national manpower. Keeping these in view, facilities for secondary education have to be extended to rural and backward areas and access provided to the weaker and more backward sections of the people, particularly the first generation learners.

A notable feature of secondary education is the mushrooming of private unaided schools in recent years. It indicates that parents are willing to pay for education that is perceived to be of good quality. The factors underlying this perception include better English teaching, better monitoring and supervision of students' performance, better attention, attendance and accountability of teachers.

In the liberalized global economy where there is a pursuit for achieving excellence, the legitimate role of private providers of quality education not only needs to be recognized, but also encouraged. Public-private-partnership (PPP) need not necessarily mean only seeking private investments to supplement governmental efforts, but also encouraging innovation in education which the government schools may lack. Schools under private management (unaided) have been expanding at a faster rate. However, a vast majority of the poor, particularly in rural areas, is solely dependent on government schools.

Secondary education should grow from the education that is being given at the primary stage, i.e. it should be closely integrated with the basic education and its essential underlying principles. There should be no wide variation in the method of teaching and curriculum of the primary and the secondary school. The planning of the secondary education must also have in view the creation of leadership in the intermediate level, because for the majority of students, formal education comes to an end at this stage. To this end, suitable types of

122 National Education Policy (NEP), 2020 and the Role of Teachers

multilateral or unilateral schools offering parallel courses should be provided and the personnel for vocational guidance should be trained. The standards to be attained should be high enough, on the one hand to make the majority of students whose education ends at the secondary stage to be efficient workers and, on the other, to enable the minority who proceed to higher education to profit from the instructions they receive at these institutions. In view of the role it has to play between the basic and the higher stage, the planning of secondary education requires considerable care and attention.

The massive expansion required in secondary education calls for an expansion in both public schools as well as private aided and unaided schools. While private schools must be allowed to expand and even encouraged, it should be noted that a much larger proportion of the expansion in enrolment has to come from the public schools.

9.1.8 Twelfth Five Year Plan (2012-17) on Secondary Education: According to Twelfth Plan, "With a dramatic growth in elementary education enrolments and improvements in retention and transition rates in recent years, particularly amongst the more disadvantaged groups, there is an increasing pressure on the secondary schools to admit more students. With the enforcement of RTE Act and further improvement in retention and transition rates, demand for secondary schooling will grow rapidly in the coming years. Meeting this demand is critical for three reasons. First, the secondary education fulfils large manpower needs of the semi-organized and the organised sectors of the economy. Second, it is the supply chain for higher education. And, finally, it caters to the needs of teachers for primary schooling. Low participation rates and poor quality at the secondary stage are a bottleneck in improving both the higher education participation and the schooling at the elementary stage.

Further, there are both social and economic benefits of secondary schooling. While there are clear improvements in health, gender equality and living conditions with secondary education, investments in secondary schooling have high marginal rates of return. Thus, the country needs to move towards universalisation of opportunity to attend secondary schooling of adequate quality. With enrolment in elementary education reaching near universal levels, there would be an opportunity to move towards universal access to secondary education. The current GER for the combined secondary and senior secondary stages (classes IX-XII) in 2009-10 at about 50 percent is woefully low. Thus, the capacity of the secondary schooling system has to be expanded significantly. There are very large inequalities in access to secondary education, by income, gender, social group and geography. The average quality of secondary education is very low. Thus, urgent efforts are needed to improve its quality. The challenge is to dramatically improve access, equity and quality of secondary education simultaneously.

India has a long tradition of partnership between the public and private sectors in secondary education. There are four types of schools: (i) government—established by State Governments (as well as some Centrally established institutions); (ii) local body—established by elected local government bodies; (iii) aided schools—private schools that receive State Government grants-in-aid and (iv) private unaided schools. Most of the growth of secondary schools in the private sector in the last two decades has occurred among unaided schools (25 percent of schools). About 60 percent of schools are now aided or unaided. It is essential, therefore, that the private sector's capabilities and potential are tapped through innovative public-private-partnerships, while concurrently stepping up public investment by the Central and State Governments at the secondary level. And given that the presence of private schools varies considerably across States, context-specific solutions need to be promoted.

While private provision in secondary education should be fostered wherever feasible, the government will have to take the prime responsibility to provide access to disadvantaged sections and to bridge the rural/urban, regional, gender and social group gaps. Simultaneously, government must invest in teacher education and accountability, curriculum reform, quality assurance, examinations reform, national assessment capabilities and management information systems, which will require time and significant institutional capacity building to succeed at a national scale". [1]

9.1.9 Recent Initiatives in School Education: These are as under:

1. **Samagra Shiksha:** It is a comprehensive programme subsuming Sarva Shiksha Abhiyan (SSA), Rashtriya Madhyamik Shiksha Abhiyan (RMSA) and Teacher Education (TE). For first time, it also includes provisions for support at pre-school level, library grants and grants for sports and physical equipment. The vision of the scheme is to ensure inclusive and equitable quality education from pre-school to senior secondary stage.

2. **Shaala Sidhi:** It enables all schools to self-evaluate their performance.

3. **E-Pathshala:** It provides digital resources such as textbooks, audio, video, periodicals etc.

4. **Saransh:** It is an initiative of CBSE for schools to conduct self-review exercises.

9.2 Vocational Education

According to National Education Policy (NEP), 2020, "vocational education is perceived to be inferior to mainstream education and meant largely for students who are unable to cope with the latter. This is a perception that affects the choices students make. It is a serious concern that can only be dealt with by a complete re-imagination of how vocational education is offered to students in the future.

This policy aims to overcome the social status hierarchy associated with vocational education and requires integration of vocational education programmes into mainstream education in all education institutions in a phased manner.

Secondary and Vocational Education

Beginning with vocational exposure at early ages in middle and secondary school, quality vocational education will be integrated smoothly into higher education. It will ensure that every child learns at least one vocation and is exposed to several more. This would lead to emphasizing the dignity of labour and importance of various vocations involving Indian arts and artisanship". [2]

Vocational training is broadly defined as training that prepares an individual for a specific vocation or occupation. Vocational education remains within the broader school curriculum and involves provision of specific skills to increase the employability of the students on completion of formal education. Vocational training is especially for a particular trade or economic activity and is conducted outside the schooling system. There are three categories of vocational education prevalent in India today: at the lower school stage, at the class 10+2 stage and at the specialised level.

Secondary education must be closely related to the psychological needs of the adolescents for whom it is being designed. In order to equip the youth adequately for the needs of the existing socio-economic situation, it is necessary to give secondary education a vocational bias. At present this education is mainly academic and does not provide sufficient scope for adolescents with varying aptitudes especially those with a marked practical bent of mind.

One of the important links between education and development is provided by manpower development through vocationalisation of secondary education related to employment. This has to be carefully designed, based on detailed surveys of existing and potential work opportunities and of available educational and training facilities. It should also keep in view the specific roles and responsibilities of the different agencies and ensure co-ordination at the operational level between the developmental programmes and the educational system. Such a differentiation should normally commence after the secondary stage and may cover varying periods depending upon the vocational area, groups of occupations and the nature and level of skills needed. It envisages deepening of practical bias in the school education to be supplemented by appropriate apprenticeship in actual field, farm or factory situations.

Vocational education and training system needs to cover more trades. Qualitatively it suffers from disabilities such as poor infrastructure, ill equipped classrooms, laboratories and workshops, non-performing faculty, absence of measurement of performance and outcomes etc. Placements are not tracked, training institutions are not rated and accreditation systems are archaic.

The Centrally-sponsored scheme of vocationalisation of secondary education at +2 level is being implemented since 1988. The revised scheme is in operation since 1992-93. The scheme provides financial assistances to States for setting up administrative structures, carrying out area-vocational surveys, preparing curriculum guides training manuals, organizing teacher training programmes, strengthening technical support system for research and development etc. It also provides financial assistance to NGOs and voluntary organisations for implementation of specific innovative projects for conducting short-term courses.

National Skill Development Mission envisages evolving a comprehensive scheme for creating a diverse and wide range of skills for youth that would enable the country to reap the scientific and demographic dividend. The emphases will be on demand-driven vocational education programmes in partnership with employers. The current programmes will be restructured with emphasis on hands-on training/exposure, vertical mobility and flexibility.

Furthermore, National Vocational Qualification Framework (NVQF) permits individuals to accumulate their knowledge and skills, and convert them through testing and certification into higher diplomas and degrees. NVQF provides quality assured various learning pathways having standards, comparable with any international qualification framework. NVQF supports lifelong learning, continuous upgradation of skills and knowledge.

National Council of Vocational Training (NCVT) designs curriculums, conducts examinations and issue certificates. States too have a counterpart organization in the State Council of Vocational Training (SCVT).

In the services sector there are two existing bodies concerned with vocational training. National Council for Hotel Management and Catering Technology (NCHM&CT) is a regulatory body for the programmes in hotel management and craft training. Construction Industry Development Council is a larger developmental body, which, *inter alia*, organizes training programmes in various trade connected with construction and even runs diploma courses in civil engineering.

9.2.1 Formal Training Programmes: Formal vocational training system demands a minimum level of education, generally higher secondary in the case of the systems co-ordinated by the Ministry of Human Resources Development (MHRD) and middle school or high school in the case of the training systems coordinated by the Ministry of Labour and Employment (MoLE), which automatically implies the exclusion of those with low levels of education. Polytechnics, under MHRD, offer diploma-level courses to meet training needs of manpower for industry at the supervisory level. The All India Council of Technical Education (AICTE) approves diploma programmes in engineering and architecture, hotel management and catering technology and pharmacy. There are 1,244 polytechnics run by MHRD with a capacity of over 2.95 lakh offerings of three-year diploma courses in various branches of engineering with an entry qualification of secondary education. Besides, there are 415 institutions for diploma in pharmacy, 63 for hotel management and 25 for architecture.

The two flagship schemes of Directorate General for Employment and Training under Ministry of Labour and Employment are the Craftsmen Training Scheme (CTS) and the Apprenticeship Training Scheme (ATS). The CTS provides institutional training whereas ATS is a combination of institutional as well as on-the-job training in which trainees are exposed to real life industrial environment. The CTS is implemented through 1987 industrial training institutes (ITIs) run by the State Governments. In addition, 4,847 industrial training centres (ITCs) in the private domain implement the CTS on the same pattern as ITIs.

A. Directorate General of Training (DGT): DGT consists of the Directorate of Training and Directorate of Apprentice Training. This includes a network of Industrial Training Institutes (ITIs) in States; Advanced Training institutes (ATIs), Regional Vocational Training Institutes (RVTIs) and other central institutes. A number of training programmes catering to students, trainers and industry requirements are being run through this network. ITIs play a vital role in the economy by providing skilled manpower in different sectors with varying levels of expertise.

9.2.2 Areas of Concern: The vocational education system suffers from deficiencies such as a low component of general education, poor linkages between the vocational education and general education streams and between the vocational education and vocational training streams. Since it creates the capability for acquiring skills, the system of general education itself, especially primary education, needs to be strengthened in the interests of skill acquisition. Education being a foundational skill, the focus on skills needs to start at the level of basic education through enlarging access and improving quality. It also needs to be noted that the link between vocational education, vocational training and actual employment is not really known, both due to the lack of actual link and due also to the paucity of information from the labour market. This has to be addressed adequately through evolving effective systems of feedback.

It is not necessary to follow a rigid sequence in the order of acquiring the several skills and it should be possible to supplement exclusive vocational training courses with necessary educational component. In this way, suitable linkages need to be established within a system for occupational mobility and career development over one's employment/working life.

Similarly, experienced craftsmen and practitioners of the arts should be used for imparting operational skills without undue insistence on pedagogic certificates. Wherever new facilities are to be created, they should be located, to the maximum extent possible, in the rural areas.

Endnotes
1. Government of India, Planning Commission, *Twelfth Five Year Plan (2012-17)*, Volume III, Chapter 21, paras 21.86 to 21.89.
2. Government of India, Ministry of Human Resource Development, *National Education Policy 2020*, p. 44.

10

Higher and Technical Education

Higher education is critical for developing a modern economy, a just society and a vibrant polity. It equips young people with skills relevant for the labour market and the opportunity for social mobility. It provides people already in employment with skills to negotiate rapidly evolving career requirements. It prepares all to be responsible citizens who value a democratic and pluralistic society. Thus, the nation creates an intellectual repository of human capital to meet the country's needs and shapes its future. Indeed, higher education is the principal site at which our national goals, developmental priorities and civic values can be examined and refined. In short, higher education is of vital importance for the country in consolidating its comparative advantage in skill- and knowledge-intensive services and in building a knowledge-based society.

10.1 Higher Education

Higher education plays an extremely important role in promoting human as well as societal wellbeing and in developing India as envisioned in its Constitution—a democratic, just, socially-conscious, cultured, and humane nation upholding liberty, equality, fraternity, and justice for all. Higher education significantly contributes towards sustainable livelihoods and economic development of the nation. As India moves towards becoming a knowledge economy and society, more and younger Indians are likely to aspire for higher education.

Given the current requirements, quality higher education must aim to develop good, thoughtful, well-rounded, and creative individuals. It must enable an individual to study one or more

Higher and Technical Education

specialized areas of interest at a deep level, and also develop character, ethical and Constitutional values, intellectual curiosity, scientific temper, creativity, spirit of service, and capabilities across a range of disciplines including sciences, social sciences, arts, humanities, languages, as well as professional, technical, and vocational subjects. A quality higher education must enable personal accomplishment and enlightenment, constructive public engagement, and productive contribution to the society. It must prepare students for more meaningful and satisfying lives and work roles and enable economic independence.

For the purpose of developing holistic individuals, it is essential that an identified set of skills and values will be incorporated at each stage of learning, from pre-school to higher education.

At the societal level, higher education must enable the development of an enlightened, socially conscious, knowledgeable, and skilled nation that can find and implement robust solutions to its own problems. Higher education must form the basis for knowledge creation and innovation thereby contributing to a growing national economy. The purpose of quality higher education is, therefore, more than the creation of greater opportunities for individual employment. It represents the key to more vibrant, socially engaged, cooperative communities and a happier, cohesive, cultured, productive, innovative, progressive, and prosperous nation.

10.1.1 Expansion of Higher Education: At the time of Independence in 1947, the number of universities was 20, of colleges around 500 and the total enrolment was around 1 lakh. The investment made in higher education over the years has given the country a strong knowledge base in many fields and contributed significantly to economic development, social progress and political democracy in independent India.

By the end of the Tenth Five Year Plan (2002-07), the Indian higher education system had grown into one of the largest in the world with 378 universities, 18,064 colleges, faculty strength of 4.92 lakh and an estimated enrolment of

140 lakh students. The higher education institutions include 23 Central universities, 216 state universities, 110 deemed universities, 11 private universities and 33 institutions of national importance established through Central legislation and another 5 institutions established through state legislations.

According to *All India Survey on Higher Education (AISHE), 2012-2013* released in 2014, in 2012-13, the number of universities stood at 665 and the number of colleges at 35,829 colleges. Of the 665 universities, 44 are central universities, 290 state public universities, 122 state private universities, 130 deemed universities, 61 institutes of national importance plus other institutes, and 5 institutions established under State Legislature Acts.

Despite the expansion that has occurred, the system is under stress to provide a sufficient volume of skilled human power, which is equipped with the required knowledge and technical skills to cater to the demands of the economy. The accelerated growth of Indian economy has already created shortages of high quality technical manpower. Though the recent emergence of the private sector in higher education has helped expand capacity, it is characterized by some imbalances. Private institutions have improved access in a few selected areas like engineering, management, medicine and IT etc. where students are willing to pay substantial fees.

10.1.2 Important Bodies for Higher Education: These are as under:

A. University Grants Commission (UGC): The UGC, a statutory body, established in 1956, operates over 100 schemes—providing a wide range of development grants to institutions, travel grants for researchers, area studies, cultural exchanges, adult education, and women studies.

The main instrument used by the UGC to obtain improvement in the standards of teaching in institutions of higher education is to require them to adhere to minimum standards in infrastructure and physical facilities and human resources as a condition for financial assistance. However,

Higher and Technical Education 133

what is needed is to induce them for striving to undertake self-improvement on a voluntary basis to obtain better standards. With this end in view, UGC in 1994 established the National Assessment and Accreditation Council (NAAC) to undertake accreditation of institutions desirous of undertaking such improvement. It is necessary to promote the process of accreditation by making available additional discretionary funds to the funding agencies to be utilised for the purpose.

B. National Assessment and Accreditation Council (NAAC): It was set up in 1994 to make quality an essential element through a combination of internal and external quality assessment and accreditation. It is an autonomous body established by the University Grants Commission (UGC) of India to assess and accredit institutions of higher education in the country. It is an outcome of the recommendations of the National Policy in Education (1986) which laid special emphasis on upholding the quality of higher education in India. To address the issues of quality, the National Policy on Education (1986) and the Plan of Action (POA-1992) advocated the establishment of an independent national accreditation body. Consequently, the NAAC was established with its headquarters in Bangalore. During the Tenth Five Year Plan (2002-07), NAAC was strengthened with the opening of 4 regional centres so as to speed up the accreditation process.

C. Academic Staff Colleges (ASCs): At present there are 66 ASCs which conduct orientation programmes of 4-weeks for newly appointed teachers and refresher courses of 3-weeks for in-service teachers. The refresher courses provide opportunities for serving teachers to learn from each other and serve as a forum for keeping abreast with the latest advances in various subjects.

D. All India Council for Technical Education (AICTE): It was given statutory status in 1987 for coordinated development of technical education, promotion of qualitative improvement and maintenance of norms and standards. AICTE has delegated the powers of approval of diploma level technical institutes to the State Governments.

Technical Education Quality Improvement Programme (TEQIP) Phase II, a four-year programme, is currently being implemented with the assistance of the World Bank, covering about 200 institutions based on competitive funding. A total of 187 institutions have been selected under TEQIP.

E. Rashtriya Uchchatar Shiksha Abhiyan (RUSA): This new mission mode scheme has been launched for strengthening and reforming higher education. It will focus on access, equity, quality, and innovation through creation, expansion and consolidation of institutions, research, and innovation and will have norm-based funding. During the Twelfth Plan, RUSA will create 80 new universities by converting autonomous colleges/colleges in a cluster to state universities, besides creating other related infrastructure.

10.1.3 Twelfth Five Year Plan (2012-17) on Higher Education: According to Twelfth Plan, "Higher education is critical for developing a modern economy, a just society and a vibrant polity. It equips young people with skills relevant for the labour market and the opportunity for social mobility. It provides people already in employment with skills to negotiate rapidly evolving career requirements. It prepares all to be responsible citizens who value a democratic and pluralistic society. Thus, the nation creates an intellectual repository of human capital to meet the country's needs and shapes its future. Indeed, higher education is the principal site at which our national goals, developmental priorities and civic values can be examined and refined.

It is estimated that developed economies and even China will face a shortage of about 40 million highly skilled workers by 2020, while, based on current projections of higher education, India is likely to see some surplus of graduates in 2020. Thus, India could capture a higher share of global knowledge-based work, for example by increasing its exports of knowledge-intensive goods and services, if there is focus on higher education and its quality is globally benchmarked. The

Higher and Technical Education 135

country cannot afford to lose time. The demographic bulge evident in India's population pyramid is encountering lower fertility rates, leading to a rapid slowdown in population growth rates and a looming decline of the population in the prime educable age up to 25 years within the next couple of decades.

Despite considerable progress during the Eleventh Plan, less than one-fifth of the estimated 120 million potential students are enrolled in higher education institutions in India, well below the world average of 26 percent. Wide disparities exist in enrolment percentages among the States and between urban and rural areas while disadvantaged sections of society and women have significantly lower enrolments than the national average. The pressure to increase access to affordable education is steadily increasing with the number of eligible students set to double by 2020. At the same time, significant problems exist in the quality of education provided. The sector is plagued by a shortage of well-trained faculty, poor infrastructure and outdated and irrelevant curricula. The use of technology in higher education remains limited and standards of research and teaching at Indian universities are far below international standards with no Indian university featured in any of the rankings of the top 200 institutions globally.

The key challenge is to find a path to achieve the divergent goals for the growth of higher education in India. Combining access with affordability and ensuring high-quality undergraduate and postgraduate education are vital for realising the potential of the country's *demographic dividend*. Future expansion should be carefully planned so as to correct regional and social imbalances, reinvigorate institutions to improve standards and reach international benchmarks of excellence, match demand with supply by improving employability, and extend the frontiers of knowledge.

The Twelfth Plan will build on the momentum generated during the Eleventh Plan and continue the focus on the three Es—expansion, equity and excellence. However, the Plan proposes a paradigm change in the way we achieve such goals—through three new principles. First, an overriding emphasis will be given to quality—as further expansion without quality improvement would be counterproductive for the future of India, given the serious quality issues noted in the sector. Second, the Plan also strives to diversify higher education opportunities, not only to meet the needs of employers, but also to offer a wide range of paths to success for our youth. India must develop world-class research universities as well as have sophisticated teaching institutions to impart key vocational and generic skills in a timely manner to cope with the rapidly changing labour market needs. Third, this excellence in diversity will be implemented through governance reforms, to enable institutions to have the autonomy to develop distinctive strengths, while being held accountable for ensuring quality.

Hence, the Twelfth Plan adopts a holistic approach to the issues of expansion, equity and excellence so that expansion is not just about accommodating ever larger number of students, but is also about providing diverse choices of subjects, levels and institutions while ensuring a minimum standard of academic quality and providing the opportunity to pursue higher education to all sections of society, particularly the disadvantaged. These objectives must guide the development of all three segments of higher education: Central institutions, which account for 2.6 percent of the total enrolment; State institutions which account for 38.5 percent of enrolment; and private institutions that cater to the remaining students. All three segments have to be expanded to achieve enrolment target by creating additional capacity and ensuring equal access opportunities, while being supported to improve the quality of teaching–learning, attain excellence in research, and contribute to economic development". [1]

Commenting on the quality of higher education and the need for improvement, Twelfth Plan observed, "The last decade has also seen a huge increase in the demand for higher education and this is expected to increase further as more children complete school and more and more jobs are seen to require higher level qualifications. However, our higher education institutions also suffer from problems of quality. Too many of our universities are producing graduates in subjects that are not required by the changing job market, and the quality is also not what it should be. Higher education policy has to be driven by three 'Es': expansion, equity and excellence.

Of these, the third E, 'excellence', is the most difficult to achieve. India cannot hope to be competitive in an increasingly knowledge driven world if our higher education institutions do not come up to the high standards of excellence needed to be able to be globally competitive. Not even one Indian university figures in the latest list of the top 200 universities in the world. We should work towards ensuring that there are at least five by the end of the Twelfth Plan. For this, universities at the top of the quality hierarchy should be identified and generously supported so that they can reach the top league. Centres of excellence within existing universities should be created. A special initiative should be launched to attract high calibre faculty from around the world on non-permanent teaching assignments". [2]

10.1.4 Problems and Policy Requirements: Higher education institutions with their research facilities are a unique base for the training of competent scientists and technologists. However, with the rapid expansion of the number of institutions and students, without the corresponding inputs by way of facilities, the role of universities as advanced centres of teaching and research has been eroded, leading not only to the weakening of science teaching and research but also adversely affecting the climate so essential for higher learning. The need, therefore, is to restore to the universities their proper image as centres of higher learning. Although it would be unrealistic to expect all the members of the academic community to take up research in addition to teaching, there is an urgent need to revive the integration of teaching and research so that universities present a different image and are restored to their recognised position.

Facilities available in universities are not adequate. That they should be increased cannot be overemphasised. It is in the general interest of universities, scientific agencies, public enterprises and technical departments in the Centre and the States, that the resources in the higher education sector are considerably augmented. The manpower that they need comes from the university sector. Moreover, as the benefits of these researches extend to several sectors of the economy, State Governments and industries should also share in funding research in universities.

Linkages between academic institutions on the one hand and national scientific agencies, laboratories and public sector enterprises on the other, have to be strengthened. This can be done in several ways such as through increased mobility of scientific personnel between education and research organisations, joint research projects, and insistence on a minimum percentage of the R&D budget of government scientific agencies and public sector enterprises being spent in the academic sector. Universities and colleges should also be encouraged to undertake applied research, useful for several regions of the country. Since the problems of a particular region are unique and intrinsic the best way that the science and technology thrust could be made in finding out solutions to those regional problems would be to make use of the local resources—people, scientists and community at large.

10.2 Technical Education

Educational programmes in the field of engineering and technology and craftsmen training—which are designed to help in building up the trained technical personnel required for schemes of industrial development, teaching and research—are immensely important. In formulating these programmes, it should be recognised that advances in the field of science and

Higher and Technical Education 139

technology will call, from time to time, for changes in patterns of training and for improvements in the system of education.

According to National Education Policy (NEP), 2020, "technical education includes degree and diploma programmes in, engineering, technology, management, architecture, town planning, pharmacy, hotel management, catering technology etc., which are critical to India's overall development. There will not only be a greater demand for well-qualified manpower in these sectors, it will also require closer collaborations between industry and higher education institutions to drive innovation and research in these fields. Furthermore, influence of technology on human endeavours is expected to erode the silos between technical education and other disciplines too. Technical education will, thus, also aim to be offered within multidisciplinary education institutions and programmes and have a renewed focus on opportunities to engage deeply with other disciplines. India must also take the lead in preparing professionals in cutting-edge areas that are fast gaining prominence, such as artificial intelligence (AI), 3-D machining, big data analysis, and machine learning, in addition to genomic studies, biotechnology, nanotechnology, neuroscience, with important applications to health, environment, and sustainable living that will be woven into undergraduate education for enhancing the employability of the youth". [3]

10.2.1 Technology and Economic Development: The pace of economic development depends on a variety of factors which constitute the psychological and sociological setting within which the economy operates. A major element in this setting is the community's will to progress and its readiness to develop and adopt new and more efficient methods and processes of production. Basically, development involves securing higher productivity all round and this is a function of the degree of technological advance the community is able to make. The problem is not one merely of adopting and applying the processes and techniques developed elsewhere, but of

140   National Education Policy (NEP), 2020 and the Role of Teachers

developing new techniques specially suited to local conditions. Modern technology is changing rapidly and no country can hope to maintain a steady pace of advance unless it keeps abreast of current developments. Techniques in turn affect and are affected by economic and social organisation. Certain forms of economic and social organisation are unsuited to or incapable of absorbing new techniques and utilising them to the best advantage. To some extent techniques must of course be adapted to economic and social organisation, but the latter has also to change in order to accommodate new techniques which need to be applied not merely in one or two isolated lines but in several lines of economic activity so that advance in one line could react on and stimulate advance in others.

The foundations of industrial and agricultural advance lie ultimately in the availability and effective use of human skills. India's Five Year Plans have emphasised the need to develop these skills at all levels. In agriculture, an integrated system involving research institutes, agricultural universities and an extension machinery has been set up. In industry, there is a network of industrial research laboratories, R&D divisions in major enterprises and consultancy firms for project consultancy and design engineering. The basis for this major advance lies in the rapid expansion of technical education.

Issues of natural resource conservation and agricultural growth cannot be effectively tackled in the absence of an appropriate technological base. In addition, technology is essential for increasing the competitiveness of the Indian economy in international markets. Indigenous development of technology is therefore of the highest importance and deliberate planned steps need to be taken to increase technological self-sufficiency of the country.

Rapid technical progress is altering fundamentally the skills, knowledge, infrastructure and institutions needed for the efficient production and delivery of goods and services. So broad and far-reaching are current technological developments that many see the emergence of another industrial revolution

Higher and Technical Education 141

driven by a new technological paradigm. This paradigm involves not only new technologies and skills in the traditional sense, but also different work methods, management techniques and organisational relations within firms. As new transport and communications technologies shrink international economic space, it also implies a significant reordering of comparative advantage, and trade and investment relations, between countries.

In India also, there is considerable technological activity in a wide spectrum of firms. What is most impressive is the number of small- and medium-sized enterprises that are investing in new technology based ventures, and often striking out in world market as exporters. However, the rest of the industrial sector still needs to invest in technology upgrading. Experience of many developing and industrialised countries suggests that a rapid acceleration of industrial technology development calls for a deliberate strategy, in the sense that it requires the government to coordinate and guide an essentially market-driven process. Free markets suffer from various kinds of market failures, they may not throw up the appropriate amounts of infrastructure, skill, information and institutional support, and mere exposure to market forces, while getting rid of inefficient policies, may not suffice to create the technological dynamism that continued industrial growth needs.

10.2.2 Technical Education Institutions in India: Technical and professional education in the country has played a significant role in economic and technical development by producing quality manpower. Strong linkages have developed between technical institutions and the industry. For strengthening technical education and improving the quality of polytechnic pass outs, various steps have been taken through technical education development programmes.

There is a widespread network of technical education institutions in India. The major among them are the following:
1. 16 Indian Institutes of Technology (IITs) and 13 Indian

Institutes of Management (IIMs), which are institutions of national importance.

2. 6,214 engineering and technology colleges and polytechnics.
3. 1,419 institutions for diploma in pharmacy.
4. 119 schools for hotel management and 165 institutions for architecture.
5. For post-graduate courses, there are 3,764 educational institutions for MBA/PGDM and 1,571 for MCA.
6. Deemed universities, namely:

- Indian Institute of Science (IISc), Bangalore.
- Indian School of Mines (ISM), Dhanbad.
- School of Planning and Architecture (SPA), New Delhi.
- Indian Institute of Information Technology and Management (IIITM), Gwalior.
- Indian Institute of Information Technology (IIIT), Allahabad.
- Indian Institute of Information Technology, Design and Manufacturing Jabalpur.

7. 30 National Institutes of Technology (NITs) which are institutions of national importance.

Tenth Five Year Plan (2002-07) saw a big increase in the number of technical and management institutions, mainly due to private initiatives. During the Tenth Plan, the number of AICTE approved degree engineering/technology institutions increased from 1,057 to 1,522 and the annual intake from 2.96 lakh to 5.83 lakh. During the Tenth Plan, University of Roorkee was upgraded to on IIT and the number of IITs increased to 7. Eleventh Five Year Plan (2007-12) envisaged setting up of 8 new IITs, 7 new IIMs and 10 new NITs. An Ordinance was promulgated for establishing 15 Central universities.

Six new Indian Institutes of Technology (IIT) started functioning in Bihar, Andhra Pradesh, Rajasthan, Odisha, Punjab and Gujarat during 2008-09. Two more IITs in Madhya Pradesh and Himachal Pradesh were expected to commence

Higher and Technical Education

their academic sessions in 2009-10.

With the commencement of academic sessions in the Indian Institutes of Science Education and Research (IISERs) at Bhopal and Thiruvananthapuram, all 5 IISERs announced by the Government are now functional.

Two new schools of planning and architecture at Vijayawada and Bhopal have already started functioning.

Teaching is expected to commence in four of the six new Indian Institutes of Management, proposed for the Eleventh Plan period, from the academic year 2009-10. These are in Haryana, Rajasthan, Jharkhand and Tamil Nadu.

As an integral part of the co-ordinated action plan for skill development, the Government created the National Skill Development Corporation in July 2008 with an initial corpus of ₹ 1,000 crore to stimulate and co-ordinate private sector participation in skill development.

The number of students in engineering and technology colleges and industrial training institutes has increased sharply. The same picture holds true for other categories like scientists, doctors and agricultural graduates.

Resultantly, India now has the third largest scientific and technical work force in the world. However, the capacity of the system to absorb fully these skills in productive employment has been less than adequate. In pure and applied research, advances have been limited except in a few areas like agricultural research, atomic energy and space. Human skills are a formidable asset since they last not merely during one working life but because they are transmitted for generations. If these assets are used effectively, they may well turn out to be one of the most fruitful results of planning.

Technical education including management education is one of the most potent means for creating skilled manpower required for developmental tasks. While this implies high costs of construction, laboratory equipment, library books and journals and high rate of obsolescence, such high cost, being directly related to development, should be viewed as an essential productive investment, yielding valuable returns to the society. The quantity of technical and management education needs to be improved not only through modernisation and upgradation of infrastructure but also by adopting futuristic approaches and strengthening industry-institutional and R&D laboratories interaction.

Indian technology policies are undergoing significant changes, and on the whole have improved greatly in recent years. A coherent technology strategy in India must address a number of interconnected elements in the incentive regime and the relevant factor markets and institutions.

10.3 Medical Education

In India, medical education is highly regulated and there is an access barrier for setting up new medical and dental colleges. Eligibility for setting up medical or dental colleges is limited to the following organizations:

1. A State Government/Union Territory.
2. A university.
3. An autonomous body promoted by Central/State Government.
4. A society registered under the Societies Registration Act, 1860 or corresponding Acts in States.
5. A public religious or charitable trust registered under the Trust Act, 1882 or the Wakf Act, 1954.

Thus, for example, the corporate sector is not eligible and only not-for-profit organizations can apply. The private sector medical and dental colleges that have been established in large numbers have all done so by setting up not-for-profit societies.

Besides the problem of the number of healthcare personnel, there is an acute problem of quality as well. Some of the private colleges are producing graduates far below the standards required but the Government colleges have also deteriorated, in part because of shortage of staff, the vacancies remaining unfilled because of unattractive remuneration. In Government medical colleges another reason for deterioration of the quality of medical graduates is that they do not get the opportunity to observe the treatment of patients because of the fall in the number of patients coming to Government hospitals for treatment.

It is often observed that Government medical colleges and hospitals are on the verge of de-recognition mainly because they fail to adhere to the infrastructure, equipment and staff norms, as laid down by Medical Council of India. This is basically due to lack of funding. Centre and States would have to make provisions for this.

In the context of medical education, the National Health Policy, 2017 observed, "The policy recommends strengthening existing medical colleges and converting district hospitals to new medical colleges to increase number of doctors and specialists, in States with large human resource deficit. The policy recognizes the need to increase the number of post graduate seats. The policy supports expanding the number of AIIMS like centres for continuous flow of faculty for medical colleges, biomedical and clinical research. National Knowledge Network shall be used for Tele-education, Tele-CME, Tele-consultations and access to digital library.

A common entrance exam is advocated on the pattern of NEET for UG entrance at All India level; a common national-level Licentiate/exit exam for all medical and nursing graduates; a regular renewal at periodic intervals with Continuing Medical Education (CME) credits accrued, are important recommendations. This policy recommends that the current pattern of MCQs (multiple choice questions) based entrance test for post-graduate medical courses—that drive students away from practical learning—should be reviewed. The policy recognizes the need to revise the under graduate and post graduate medical curriculum keeping in view the changing needs, technology and the newer emerging disease trends. Keeping in view, the rapid expansion of medical colleges in public and private sector there is an urgent need to review existing institutional mechanisms to regulate and ensure quality of training and education being imparted. The policy recommends that the discussion on recreating a regulatory structure for health professional education be revisited to address the emerging needs and challenges". [4]

10.4 Areas of Concern

A critical overview of higher education in India brings out a number of issues. Chief among them are the deterioration in quality, the resource crunch leading to poor infrastructure and the serious problems of governance brought about by the influence of factors and forces extraneous to educational objectives.

10.4.1 Private Sector Institutions: Recent decades have seen the emergence of private sector institutions, particularly in technical education, financed by large capitation fees charged by them. This development has been inequitable, as it has led to the deprivation of a large number of students who have not been able to pay the substantial sums involved in the capitation fees. While encouraging private sector initiative to expand higher education, it has become necessary for the Government to ensure that private sector institutions take measures to provide scholarships and free-ships to an adequate number of meritorious students who do not have the means to pay the fees.

10.4.2 Shortage of Faculty: One of the main reasons for falling standards of higher education is the teacher shortage in the institutions of higher learning, particularly the technical education institutions. The salaries commanded by graduates in the market are so high that they do not have the motivation to move on for post-graduation or doctoral level with the ultimate objective of becoming teachers. In order to make the teaching profession attractive and motivate bright young professionals to take post-graduate courses, it is necessary to look at the salary structure and career opportunities of teachers in colleges. Research project funds must be shared as incentive payment to the faculty and the faculty should be given maximum freedom to undertake consultancies.

10.4.3 Curricula and Assessment: The decline in standards in higher education is also due to the failure to revise the curricula to keep pace with the developments in the various fields of knowledge as well in the society. The curricula must be revised every three years and the revisions must be subjected to outside peer review. The process of revision should be streamlined and decentralised with more autonomy given to teachers.

One of the major reforms needed in the education system is a change in the method of assessment of students, which relies exclusively on examinations. The current system is inadequate because it tests memory rather than understanding and does not encourage the development of analytical and creative abilities. Assessment of students must be based on the work done throughout the year rather than being judged solely on the performance during the annual examination. Evaluation of courses and teachers by students should also be used as an input in the process of assessment of students. Semester system must be introduced in the institutions of higher education. Also important is the need to introduce a system of credits whereby a student who discontinues studies or who changes institutions may be granted recognition for the courses completed earlier, thus granting them spatial and temporal flexibility in pursuing studies.

10.4.4 Non-viable Institutions: The problem of non-viable institutions, with low enrolment and inadequate provision of facilities, as well as proliferation of such institutions, offering general academic courses, would need to be tackled with determination, both in order to avoid increasing unemployment among the graduates as well as to make better use of the available economic resources for educational development. At the same time, the problems of first generation learners, particularly the socially disadvantaged sections—for whom higher education provides a transition, opportunity and challenge in terms of life perspectives and socio-economic aspirations of the community—

148 National Education Policy (NEP), 2020 and the Role of Teachers

would need to be harmonized into the academic pattern.

To sum up, the problem of the re-organisation of university education is really three-fold: the reform of the existing system to enable it to yield the best results it is capable of yielding, the building up of a new system (or systems) more suited to national needs and the working out of the relationship of the various systems, while they exist side by side. In spite of their grave defects, the existing universities are the only repositories of the tradition of organised knowledge and the course of wisdom is to improve their working while building a better system is attempted.

Extensive and widespread facilities have already been created for higher education and the main thrust should be to co-ordinate them and maximise their utilisation. There is sufficient scope for, and possibility of, greater use of the infrastructural physical facilities. The existing imbalances in the level of development of universities among themselves as well as in relation to colleges would have to be examined for suitable remedial programmes and selective support in keeping with their requirements, potential and scope.

Higher education needs to be extended in an equitable and cost-effective manner mainly by large-scale expansion of distance education system and increased involvement of voluntary and private agencies. Apart from strengthening of facilities and restructuring curriculum, the component of value education should be introduced as part of foundation programme. While an integrated approach to the development of higher education needs to be adopted, measures to promote excellence should be emphasised.

The excellence of India's university products and professionals is well acknowledged, both at home and abroad. The competitive advantage of the country can be maintained and improved only if the university and higher education sectors perform well. Their contribution to improving capability to interact effectively with the fast expanding global techno-economic systems has been significant and their

Higher and Technical Education 149

potential needs to be harnessed to the full.

One of the major reforms needed in the education system is a change in the method of assessment of students, which relies exclusively on examinations. The current system is inadequate because it tests memory rather than understanding and does not encourage the development of analytical and creative abilities. Assessment of students must be based on the work done throughout the year rather than being judged solely on the performance during the annual examination. Evaluation of courses and teachers by students should also be used as an input in the process of assessment of students. Semester system must be introduced in the institutions of higher education. Also important is the need to introduce a system of credits whereby a student who discontinues studies or who changes institutions may be granted recognition for the courses completed earlier, thus granting them spatial and temporal flexibility in pursuing studies.

10.5 National Education Policy (NEP), 2020 on Higher Education

NEP, 2020 has listed the following major problems currently faced by the higher education system in India:

1. "A severely fragmented higher educational ecosystem.
2. Less emphasis on the development of cognitive skills and learning outcomes.
3. A rigid separation of disciplines, with early specialisation and streaming of students into narrow areas of study.
4. Limited access particularly in socio-economically disadvantaged areas, with few HEIs that teach in local languages.
5. Limited teacher and institutional autonomy.
6. Inadequate mechanisms for merit-based career management and progression of faculty and institutional leaders.
7. Lesser emphasis on research at most universities and colleges, and lack of competitive peer-reviewed research

funding across disciplines.
8. Suboptimal governance and leadership of HEIs.
9. An ineffective regulatory system.
10. Large affiliating universities resulting in low standards of undergraduate education". [5]

NEP, 2020 envisions a complete overhaul and re-energising of the higher education system to overcome these challenges and thereby deliver high-quality higher education, with equity and inclusion. The vision of NEP, 2020 includes the following key changes to the current system:

1. "Moving towards a higher educational system consisting of large, multidisciplinary universities and colleges, with at least one in or near every district, and with more HEIs across India that offer medium of instruction or programmes in local/Indian languages.
2. Moving towards a more multidisciplinary undergraduate education.
3. Moving towards faculty and institutional autonomy.
4. Revamping curriculum, pedagogy, assessment, and student support for enhanced student experiences.
5. Reaffirming the integrity of faculty and institutional leadership positions through merit appointments and career progression based on teaching, research, and service.
6. Establishment of a National Research Foundation to fund outstanding peer-reviewed research and to actively seed research in universities and colleges.
7. Governance of HEIs by high qualified independent boards having academic and administrative autonomy.
8. *Light but tight* regulation by a single regulator for higher education.
9. Increased access, equity, and inclusion through a range of measures, including greater opportunities for outstanding public education; scholarships by private/philanthropic universities for disadvantaged and underprivileged students; online education, and open distance learning

(ODL); and all infrastructure and learning materials accessible and available to learners with disabilities". [6]

Endnotes

1. Government of India, Planning Commission, *Twelfth Five Year Plan (2012-17)*, Volume III, Chapter 21, paras 21.180 to 21.185.
2. Government of India, Planning Commission, *Twelfth Five Year Plan (2012-17)*, Volume I, Chapter 1, para 1.53.
3. Government of India, Ministry of Human Resource Development, *National Education Policy 2020*, p. 51.
4. Government of India, Ministry of Heath and Family Welfare, *National Health Policy, 2017*, p. 16.
5. *National Education Policy 2020*, op. cit., p. 33.
6. Ibid., p. 34.

11

Education and Skill Development

Education and skill development are necessary to meet the needs of a growing economy and to promote social equality by empowering those currently excluded because of unequal access to education and skills to participate fully in the growth process.

Occupational patterns are changing; and new jobs and job titles, job enlargement, job enrichment, and new flexible work arrangements are emerging. Employment demands are shifting towards higher skill categories. It is imperative, therefore, for India to move up the skill-ladder and produce a larger number of people with higher education and generic training for new types of knowledge work, both in high skill services and high technology industrial production. Knowledge professionals will need support from middle-skilled workers in new knowledge and technology areas. The skill development system will need to meet this challenge. The response time is limited as the rate of change is high and accelerating.

11.1 Meaning and Importance of Skill Development

The term *skill* is used in the literature to refer to a wide range of attributes and to that extent there is no clear definition of a skilled worker. In practical terms, the term used is *marketable skill* which commonly refers to any skill/expertise/ability that has a market value, i.e. which has the potential of being utilised for generating income/employment.

Skill development is important because of its contribution to enhancing productivity at the individual, industry and also national levels because of the complementarities that exist between physical capital and human capital on the one hand and between technology and human capital on the other. Fast

Education and Skill Development 153

changing knowledge economies call for new core competencies among all learners in the society.

In short, skills are at the core of improving employment outcomes of individuals and increasing productivity and growth of countries. This is particularly relevant as today's developing and emerging countries seek higher sustained growth rates. Most of them face serious demographic challenges, including "youth bulge" of new jobseekers.

In many countries, education systems are not providing young people with the basic skills that make them *trainable*. And serious handicaps are inflicted early in life when children are malnourished or insufficiently stimulated. Moreover, rigid labour markets in many countries reduce mobility and make it difficult for workers to find jobs—and for firms to find the right workers.

In this context, it is indispensable to have the following comprehensive and adaptive systems to build skills.

1. Right start for children.
2. Ensuring that all students learn.
3. Job-relevant skills.
4. Entrepreneurship and innovation.
5. Matching supply of skills with demand.
6. Technological upgradation.

Schools are expected to teach basic competencies that enable students to acquire the skills that would help them make informed life choices and that would later be valued by employers and useful for self-employment. In fact, the seeds of these competencies should have been planted from infancy, and schools should develop them. These competencies include the following:

1. Problem-solving skills.
2. Learning skills.
3. Communication skills.
4. Personal skills.
5. Social skills.

In addition to these basic competencies, skills that are more directly required for work can be developed through schooling:

11.2 Job-relevant Skills

Job-relevant skills refer to a set of competencies valued by employers and useful for self-employment. They include skills relevant to the specific job of the worker as well as other skills that enhance his or her productivity. These other skills include the following:

1. Problem-solving skills or the capacity to think critically and analyze.
2. Learning skills or the ability to acquire new knowledge ("learning to learn"), distil lessons from experience, and apply them in search of innovations.
3. Communication skills, including reading and writing, collecting and using information to communicate with others, and using a foreign language and information and communication technologies (ICTs) as communication tools.
4. Personal skills for self-management, making sound judgments, and managing risks.
5. Social skills to collaborate with and motivate others in a team, manage client relations, exercise leadership, resolve conflicts, and develop social networks.

Because country conditions differ, there is no ideal reform package to balance the supply of skills imparted through pre-employment training programs and the employer demand for skills. The challenge is creating the environment for providers of training to have the incentives to respond to the needs of the labour market.

Perhaps the most frequent complaint, especially about public institutions that offer technical and vocational education and training (TVET), is that the system produces the same graduates year after year with little regard to labour market signals. In addition, costs are high, public support is weak for what is considered a poor route to jobs, and the curriculum is often narrowly geared toward jobs in the formal sector, which

Education and Skill Development 155

in most low-income countries is tiny and not growing fast enough to offer many new jobs.

11.3 On-the-job Training (OJT)

OJT contributes much to the stock of human capital, with estimates ranging from a quarter to half of all human capital formation in the United States. It tends to favour workers with higher levels of educational attainment and occurs more frequently in larger firms and in more dynamic, export-oriented sectors. The bias often puts countries in a paradox, with firms complaining about skill shortages while also being unwilling or unable to upgrade their own workers' skills through OJT.

(TVET) programmes are highly diverse in the competencies they impart. Their entry requirements also vary greatly, from the fairly modest (courses on simple welding jobs), to the moderately demanding (courses for tool and die makers, aerospace-certified welders, air traffic controllers, high voltage technicians), to the highly demanding (courses for engineers, designers, scientists, neurosurgeons).

The diversity implies that training occurs in a correspondingly wide variety of settings: in schools that offer TVET courses and in post-secondary institutions such as community colleges, polytechnics, universities and other specialized institutes (and indeed in overseas institutions in esoteric fields). The courses offered at universities are generally viewed as professional training rather than TVET; the training of teachers (and sometimes that of health workers, including doctors) is treated likewise. The term TVET is thus often used tacitly to refer to the training of other workers, with vocational training typically assumed to be geared to trainees expecting jobs as skilled workers at the lower to mid-level, and technical training mostly directed at those aiming for skilled jobs at higher levels of responsibility.

11.4 Matching Supply of Skills with Demand

Even if individuals have the "right" skills to be productive

156 National Education Policy (NEP), 2020 and the Role of Teachers

and creative, employment and productivity can be hampered if labour markets do not function well. Employers need the flexibility to manage their human resources. Workers need to move freely between jobs and regions. And employers have to find the skills they need, and workers the jobs that put their skills to best use. When workers cannot move freely, both output and productivity growth are reduced.

Youths entering the labour market for the first time, and thus lacking work experience and professional references, are likely to face more difficulties signalling their skills to potential employers. This problem can be amplified when there is no proper certification or accreditation for different training centres or universities. Indeed, there is some evidence that the transition to stable formal jobs involves a period where young workers alternate between short-term/low productivity jobs in the informal sector. The problem is likely to be even more severe for informal sector workers lacking university or training diplomas.

Governments can facilitate labour mobility and job searches through various interventions, including a better combination of job and income protection policies and more proactive approaches to employment services and skills certification. The other side of the coin in efforts to enhance labour mobility involves expanding coverage of social protection systems to protect workers' incomes in the face of job loss. In many cases, innovations in income protection systems can provide an alternative to expensive severance pay systems—thus better protecting workers while facilitating mobility.

In fact, employment services are being revamped in several middle-income countries. International experience shows what's important for the successful design of these programmes:

1. Providing incentives for job-seekers and employers to join.
2. Integrating employment services with training and competency assessment programs.

Education and Skill Development 157

3. Decentralizing management and expanding the role of the private sector with clear targets.
4. Exploiting information technologies.

Skills are at the core of improving individuals' employment outcomes and increasing countries' productivity and growth. This is particularly relevant as today's developing and emerging countries seek higher sustained growth rates.

11.5 System of Skill Development in India

In India, skill formation is broadly through general education as a provider of generic skills. Vocational education and training provide marketable industry specific skills for better employability. Other than general education, skill formation efforts consist of the following: (a) vocational education, (b) vocational training and (c) sector-specific programmes to address the issues of skill formation and enhancement.

Within vocational training, distinction can be made between the formal and the informal streams both of which take place under the aegis of the government as well as the private and non-government agencies. Broadly, the following four systems cater to the training needs: (a) the governmental formal training system, (b) the governmental system that focuses exclusively on the informal sector, (c) non-governmental (private as well as NGO) network of formal training institutions and (d) the non-governmental (mostly NGO-led) principally non-formal training programmes for the informal sector.

Skill development programmes are undertaken by various ministries and departments, commissions, councils, autonomous bodies and institutions as well as public-private-partnership bodies. Ministry of Skill Development and Entrepreneurship (MSDE), Ministry of Human Resources Development, and Ministry of Labour and Employment are the three major ministries responsible for skill development. Most of the initiatives by other ministries/departments are sectoral in nature

158   National Education Policy (NEP), 2020 and the Role of Teachers

and target group oriented.

Most of these schemes and programmes are administered at the field level by the departments and agencies of the respective State Governments or other non-government organisations identified for the purpose. The funds flow downwards and the State Governments are usually assigned the task of implementing as well as monitoring the skill formation programmes on a routine basis. Alternatively, the Central Government departments entrust a number of their programmes directly to non-government organisations. This sometimes results in overlapping of efforts in the implementation of the programmes.

11.5.1 Private Sector Initiatives for Skill Building: Private sector initiatives can be broadly categorised into the following four types: (a) where private entrepreneurs or corporations establish training centres/institutes on a for-profit basis, (b) where private corporations impart training to people who get absorbed as skilled workforce in their own units, (c) where they enter into partnerships with public agencies and become the vehicles for training delivery and sometimes finance and (d) where corporate houses set up public trusts or foundations with a development agenda to build the capacities of local communities to be self-reliant and create systems that utilize human and physical capital in a sustainable manner as an integral part of their corporate social responsibility (CSR) mandate.

Private sector initiatives in skill building tend to be more linked to industry demand and hence avoid the wastages associated with supply-led initiatives. However, these are likely to be forthcoming only in response to existing demand and where skilling is likely to have a direct link with profitability. For a large segment of workers in the informal sector, these considerations are not enough and their skilling needs go far beyond those that are likely to be addressed directly by the private sector.

11.5.2 Initiatives of NGOs in Skill Building: NGOs interventions range from offering formal ITI courses

Education and Skill Development 159

[approved by National Council for Vocational Training (NCVT)] to a wide range of non-formal courses. Typically, NGOs devise their own curricula, provide their own training and have their own certification procedures. Very often, they have contacts with employers in the neighbouring areas which provide placements for the trainees. It is often also reported that placement in jobs for those trained are high and that trained workers earn higher wages. There are two types of approaches being followed: (a) training only on basic or upgraded skills and then leave the trainees to seek wage employment or start their own enterprises and (b) a *holistic* package of skill development, basic entrepreneurship training and assistance in availing credit facilities etc. Some NGOs even *handhold* the trainees for a certain period.

Thus, the non-government initiatives, whether by the private sector or by NGOs, address some of the deficiencies that exist in existing government-led systems. They provide training that is demand-led with signals being provided by the market. NGOs adopt a more integrated approach, with different emphasis across different kinds of organisations, but their interventions are too small and dispersed to make a significant difference in terms of the number of workers trained. Further, they suffer from the problems of inconsistent curriculum, lack of certification and standardisation.

11.6 Special Target Groups for Skill Development

One of the biggest challenges of skill development in our country is that 93 percent of the workforce is in the unorganized/informal sector. Consequently it is difficult to map existing skills in the unorganised sector and gauge the skilling requirement in the sector. On the other hand, the rate of job growth in informal sector is estimated to be twice that in formal sector.

Women constitute almost half of the demographic dividend. The key challenge here is to increase their participation in the country's labour force, which is directly linked to economic

160   National Education Policy (NEP), 2020 and the Role of Teachers

growth of the country. Mainstreaming gender roles by skilling women in non-traditional roles and increasing gender sensitivity in the workplace will have a catalytic effect on productivity.

The target groups in the unorganized sector include, among others, the following:

1. Own-account workers.
2. Workers and apprentices in micro enterprises.
3. Unpaid family workers.
4. Casual labourers.
5. Home-based workers.
6. Peripatetic workers.
7. Migrant labourers.
8. Out of school youth and adults in need of skills.
9. Farmers and artisans in rural areas.

In order to encourage participation in skill development, entry barriers such as educational qualification, transportation, loss of wages, problem of language etc. should be suitably addressed.

11.7 Skill Development for Women Workers

Skill development for employability should be used as an agent of change in promoting women's employment. Women face a multitude of barriers in accessing skills and productive employment, remaining on the job due to effect of globalization or otherwise and advancing to higher level jobs, as well as returning to the labour market after a period of absence, for example, in raising children. A policy of non-discrimination needs to be pursued vigorously to provide equal access for women to skill development and employment.

The problems of women workers in general and in the unorganised sector in particular deserve special emphasis and focus in view of their marginalised position within the class of workers. Even when women are not employed in the sense of contributing to the national output, a considerable share of their time is consumed by socially productive and reproductive labour. This is what is called the *double burden of work* that distinguishes women from men. For women workers in the informal economy, the double burden of combining the tasks of production and reproduction is even more arduous because they are already engaged in activities that require long hours to obtain a subsistence wage.

Thus, while women workers constitute a marginalised category within the class of workers in general, there are layers of subordination determined by structural factors such as the initial conditions of social status and economic sector to which they belong. This is quite evident in the case of women workers in the unorganised sector. There is greater disadvantage for women workers in general and those belonging to rural as well as scheduled castes (SCs)/scheduled tribes (STs) in particular. Apart from such inherited disadvantages as lower social position, a number of other factors also contribute to such a picture. These are their limited asset position, access to resources, and low level of education and skill. Education, and consequently some ability to acquire formal skills, could be a moderating force but this aspect presents a dismal picture. The overall situation of women workers calls for interventions of a promotional nature from different entry points but with a strong emphasis on education.

11.8 National Policy for Skill Development and Entrepreneurship (NPSDE), 2015

The Ministry of Labour and Employment, Government of India, had formulated a National Policy on Skill Development in 2009. The objective of this policy was to empower all individuals through improved skills, knowledge, nationally and internationally recognized qualifications to gain access to decent employment and ensure India's competitiveness in the global market.

On July 15, 2015, Prime Minister Narendra Modi launched the National Policy for Skill Development and Entrepreneurship (NPSDE), 2015 along with the following three other landmark initiatives of the Ministry of Skill Development and Entrepreneurship:

162 National Education Policy (NEP), 2020 and the Role of Teachers

1. National Skill Development Mission.
2. Pradhan Mantri Kaushal Vikas Yojana (PMKVY).
3. Skill Loan Scheme.

The 2009 policy was, thus, superseded by NPSDE, 2015. The new policy tries to bring the world of education and training closer to the world of work so as to enable them together build a strong India.

The Ministry of Skill Development and Entrepreneurship, Government of India, is an integral part of the government policy on *Sabka Saath, Sabka Vikaas* and its commitment to overall human resources development to take advantage of the demographic profile of India in the coming years. The objective of NPSDE, 2015 is to meet the challenge of skilling at scale with speed and standard (quality). It aims to provide an umbrella framework to all skilling activities being carried out within the country, and to align them to common standards and link the skilling with demand centres.

In addition to laying down the objectives and expected outcomes, it also identifies the various institutional frameworks which can act as the vehicle to reach the expected outcomes. The national policy also provides clarity and coherence on how skill development efforts across the country can be aligned within the existing institutional arrangements. This policy links skills development to improved employability and productivity.

The salient features and provisions of NPSDE, 2015 are presented below.

11.8.1 Vision and Mission:

Vision: To create an ecosystem of empowerment by skilling on a large scale at speed with high standards and to promote a culture of innovation based entrepreneurship which can generate wealth and employment so as to ensure Sustainable livelihoods for all citizens in the country.

Mission: The mission is to:
1. Create a demand for skilling across the country.
2. Correct and align skilling with required competencies.
3. Connect the supply of skilled human resources with

sectoral demands.

4. Certify and assess in alignment with global and national standards.

5. Catalyse an ecosystem wherein productive and innovative entrepreneurship germinates, sustains and grows leading to creation of a more dynamic entrepreneurial economy and more formal wage employment.

11.8.2 Objectives of NPSDE, 2015: The core objective of NPSDE, 2015 is to empower the individuals by enabling them to realize their full potential through a process of lifelong learning where competencies are accumulated via instruments such as credible certifications, credit accumulation and transfer etc. As individuals grow, the society and nation also benefit from their productivity and growth. This will involve the following:

1. Make quality vocational training aspirational for both youth and employers whereby youth sees it as a matter of choice and employer acknowledges the productivity linked to skilled workforce by paying the requisite premium.

2. Ensure both vertical and horizontal pathways to skilled workforce for further growth by providing seamless integration of skill training with formal education.

3. Focus on an outcome-based approach towards quality skilling that on the one hand results in increased employability and better livelihoods for individuals, and on the other hand translates into improved productivity across primary, secondary and tertiary sectors.

4. Increase the capacity and quality of training infrastructure and trainers to ensure equitable and easy access to every citizen.

5. Address human resources needs by aligning supply of skilled workers with sectoral requirements of industry and the country's strategic priorities including flagship programmes like 'Make in India'.

6. Establish an IT-based information system for aggregating demand and supply of skilled workforce which can help in

164 National Education Policy (NEP), 2020 and the Role of Teachers

matching and connecting supply with demand.

7. Promote national standards in the skilling space through active involvement of employers in setting occupational standards, helping develop curriculum, providing apprenticeship opportunities, participating in assessments, and providing gainful employment to skilled workforce with adequate compensation. Operationalize a well-defined quality assurance framework aligned with global standards to facilitate mobility of labour.

8. Leverage modern technology to ensure scale, access and outreach, in addition to ease of delivering content and monitoring results.

9. Recognise the value of on-the-job training, by making apprenticeships in actual work environments an integral part of all skill development efforts.

10. Ensure that the skilling needs of the socially and geographically disadvantaged and marginalized groups—like the scheduled castes (SCs), scheduled tribes (STs), other backward classes (OBCs), minorities, differently-abled persons—are appropriately taken care of.

11. Promote increased participation of women in the workforce through appropriate skilling and gender mainstreaming of training.

12. Promote commitment and ownership of all stakeholders towards skill development and create an effective coordination mechanism.

The core objective of the entrepreneurship framework is to coordinate and strengthen factors essential for growth of entrepreneurship across the country. This would include as under:

1. Promote entrepreneurship culture and make it aspirational.

2. Encourage entrepreneurship as a viable career option through advocacy.

3. Enhance support for potential entrepreneurs through mentorship and networks.

4. Integrate entrepreneurship education in the formal

education system.

5. Foster innovation-driven and social entrepreneurship to address the needs of the population at the *bottom of the pyramid*.

6. Ensure ease of doing business by reducing entry and exit barriers.

7. Facilitate access to finance through credit and market linkages.

8. Promote entrepreneurship amongst women.

9. Broaden the base of entrepreneurial supply by meeting specific needs of both socially and geographically disadvantaged sections of the society including SCs, STs, OBCs, minorities, differently-abled persons.

11.9 National Skill Development Mission (NSDM), 2015

Skills and knowledge are the driving forces of economic growth and social development for any country. India currently faces a severe shortage of well-trained, skilled workers. It is estimated that only 2.3 percent of the workforce in India has undergone formal skill training as compared to 68 percent in the UK, 75 percent in Germany, 52 percent in USA, 80 percent in Japan and 96 percent in South Korea. [1]

Large sections of the educated workforce have little or no job skills, making them largely unemployable. Therefore, India must focus on scaling up skill training efforts to meet the demands of employers and drive economic growth.

This demographic advantage is predicted to last only until 2040. India therefore has a very narrow timeframe to harness its demographic dividend and to overcome its skill shortages. The enormity of India's skilling challenge is further aggravated by the fact that skill training efforts cut across multiple sectors and require the involvement of diverse stakeholders such as: (a) multiple government departments at the centre and state levels, (b) private training providers, (c) educational and training institutions, (d) employers, (e) industry associations and (f) assessment and certification

166   National Education Policy (NEP), 2020 and the Role of Teachers

bodies and trainees. All these stakeholders need to align their work together in order to achieve the target of Skill India.

National Skill Development Mission (NSDM) was approved by the Union Cabinet on July 1, 2015, and officially launched by the Prime Minister on July 15, 2015 on the occasion of World Youth Skills Day. 18,000 plus ITI graduating students received job offer letters on the occasion of World Youth Skills Day. Government has set a target to provide skill training to 40.02 crore people by 2022.

NSDM has been developed to create convergence across sectors and States in terms of skill training activities. Further, to achieve the vision of Skilled India, NSDM would not only consolidate and co-ordinate skilling efforts, but also expedite decision making across sectors to achieve skilling at scale with speed and standards. It will be implemented through a streamlined institutional mechanism driven by Ministry of Skill Development and Entrepreneurship (MSDE).

The Ministry of Skill Development and Entrepreneurship (earlier Department of Skill Development and Entrepreneurship, first created in July 2014) was set up in November 2014 to drive the Skill India agenda in a Mission Mode in order to converge existing skill training initiatives and combine scale and quality of skilling efforts, with speed.

The Ministry, therefore, launched NSDM which will provide the overall institutional framework to rapidly implement and scale up skill development efforts across India. It seeks to provide the institutional capacity to train a minimum of 300 million skilled people by the year 2022.

11.9.1 Objectives of NSDM: NSDM seeks to:

1. Create an end-to-end implementation framework for skill development, which provides opportunities for life-long learning. This includes incorporation of skilling in the school curriculum, providing opportunities for quality long and short-term skill training, by providing gainful employment and ensuring career progression that meets the aspirations of trainees.

Education and Skill Development   167

2. Align employer/industry demand and workforce productivity with trainees' aspirations for sustainable livelihoods, by creating a framework for outcome focused training.

3. Establish and enforce cross-sectoral, nationally and internationally acceptable standards for skill training in the country by creating a sound quality assurance framework for skilling, applicable to all Ministries, States and private training providers.

4. Build capacity for skill development in critical unorganized sectors (such as the construction sector, where there are few opportunities for skill training) and provide pathways for re-skilling and up-skilling workers in these identified sectors, to enable them to transition into formal sector employment.

5. Ensure sufficient, high quality options for long-term skilling, benchmarked to internationally acceptable qualification standards, which will ultimately contribute to the creation of a highly skilled workforce.

6. Develop a network of quality instructors/trainers in the skill development ecosystem by establishing high quality teacher training institutions.

7. Leverage existing public infrastructure and industry facilities for scaling up skill training and capacity building efforts.

8. Offer a passage for overseas employment through specific programmes mapped to global job requirements and benchmarked to international standards.

9. Enable pathways for transitioning between the vocational training system and the formal education system, through a credit transfer system.

10. Promote convergence and co-ordination between skill development efforts of all Central Ministries, Departments, States, and implementing agencies.

11. Support weaker and disadvantaged sections of society through focused outreach programmes and targeted skill development activities.

168   National Education Policy (NEP), 2020 and the Role of Teachers

12. Propagate aspirational value of skilling among youth, by creating social awareness on value of skill training.
13. Maintain a national database, known as the Labour Market Information System (LMIS), which will act as a portal for matching the demand and supply of skilled workforce in the country. The LMIS, will on the one hand provide citizens with vital information on skilling initiatives across the country. On the other, it will also serve as a platform for monitoring the performance of existing skill development programmes, running in every Indian state.

11.9.2 Institutional Mechanisms: Key institutional mechanisms for achieving the objectives of NSDM have been divided into three tiers. NSDM will consist of a Governing Council at apex level, a Steering Committee, and a Mission Directorate as the executive arm of the Mission.

Mission Directorate will be supported by three other institutions: National Skill Development Agency (NSDA), National Skill Development Corporation (NSDC), and Directorate General of Training (DGT)—all of which will have linkages with Mission Directorate to facilitate smooth functioning of the national institutional mechanism. These three agencies would continue to lie under the umbrella of Ministry of Skill Development and Entrepreneurship.

At State level, States will be encouraged to create State Skill Development Missions (SSDM) along the lines of National Skill Development Mission with a Steering Committee and Mission Directorate at State level. States will, in turn, be supported by District Committees at the functional tier.

11.9.3 NSDM Strategy: Seven sub-missions have been proposed initially to act as building blocks for achieving overall objectives of NSDM. They are:

1. Institutional training.
2. Infrastructure.
3. Convergence.
4. Trainers.
5. Overseas employment.

Education and Skill Development 169

6. Sustainable livelihoods.
7. Leveraging public infrastructure.

The sub-missions can be added to/amended as per decision of Governing Council. The power to identify sub-missions in crucial areas which require immediate attention will lie with Governing Council chaired by the Prime Minister. Executive guidelines and detailing of each sub-mission will be done by Executive Committee headed by Secretary, MSDE.

Key focus areas of the sub-missions include: (a) addressing the long-term and short-term skilling needs through revamp of existing institutional training framework and establishing new institutions, (b) undertaking sector-specific skill training initiatives, (c) ensuring convergence of existing skill development programmes, (d) leveraging existing public infrastructure for skilling, (e) focusing on training of trainers, (f) facilitating overseas employment, and (g) promoting sustainable livelihoods.

Sub-Missions have currently been proposed in priority areas. The number of sub-missions can be modified as per changing skill requirements and challenges. Each sub-mission will be headed by a Joint Secretary or Director level officer designated as CEO, sourced from the public or private sector, who has a solid track record of implementing projects and achieving targets in a timely manner. The Sub-Mission's support team will consist of high performing individuals drawn from the public and private domains.

11.10 Pradhan Mantri Kaushal Vikas Yojana (PMKVY)

On July 15, 2015, Prime Minister Narendra Modi launched the Pradhan Mantri Kaushal Vikas Yojana (PMKVY). The slogan *Kaushal Bharat, Kushal Bharat* suggests that skilling Indians (*Kaushal Bharat*) will result in a happy, healthy, prosperous and strong nation (*Kushal Bharat*).

PMKVY is the flagship, demand-driven, reward-based skill training scheme of the Ministry of Skill Development and Entrepreneurship (MSDE). It is intended to incentivise skill

170 National Education Policy (NEP), 2020 and the Role of Teachers

training by providing financial rewards to candidates who successfully complete approved skill training programmes. For the first time, the skills of young people who lack formal certification, such as workers in India's vast unorganised sector, will be recognised. Through an initiative known as recognition of prior learning (RPL), 10 lakh youth will be assessed and certified for the skills that they already possess.

Under PMKVY, skill cards and skill certificates are awarded which allow trainees to share their skill identity with employers. Each skill card and skill certificate features a quick response code (QR Code), which can be read through a QR reader on mobile devices. Trainees can use these to share their skill qualifications with employers in a quick and reliable way during the job search process.

Approved for another four years (2016-2020) to benefit 10 million youth, training and assessment fees under PMKVY are completely paid by the Government.

11.10.1 Key Components of the Scheme: These are as under:

A. Short-term Training: Short-term training imparted at PMKVY Training Centres (TCs) is expected to benefit candidates of Indian nationality who are either school/college dropouts or unemployed. Apart from providing training according to the National Skills Qualification Framework (NSQF), TCs shall also impart training in soft skills, entrepreneurship, financial and digital literacy. Duration of the training varies per job role, ranging between 150 and 300 hours. Upon successful completion of their assessment, candidates shall be provided placement assistance by Training Partners (TPs). Under PMKVY, the entire training and assessment fees are paid by the Government. Payouts shall be provided to the TPs in alignment with the Common Norms. Trainings imparted under the short-term training component of the scheme shall be NSQF Level 5 and below.

B. Recognition of Prior Learning: Individuals with prior learning experience or skills shall be assessed and certified

Education and Skill Development 171

under the Recognition of Prior Learning (RPL) component of the scheme. RPL aims to align the competencies of the unregulated workforce of the country to the NSQF. Project Implementing Agencies (PIAs), such as Sector Skill Councils (SSCs) or any other agencies designated by MSDE/NSDC, shall be incentivized to implement RPL projects in any of the three project types (RPL Camps, RPL at Employers Premises and RPL Centres). To address knowledge gaps, PIAs may offer Bridge Courses to RPL candidates.

11.10.2 Special Projects: The special projects component of PMKVY envisages the creation of a platform that will facilitate trainings in special areas and/or premises of Government bodies, corporates or industry bodies, and trainings in special job roles not defined under the available Qualification Packs (QPs)/National Occupational Standards (NOSs). Special projects are projects that require some deviation from the terms and conditions of short-term training under PMKVY for any stakeholder. A proposing stakeholder can be either Government institutions of Central and State Government(s)/Autonomous Body/Statutory Body or any other equivalent body or corporates who desire to provide training to candidates.

11.10.3 Kaushal and Rozgar Mela: Social and community mobilisation is extremely critical for the success of PMKVY. Active participation of the community ensures transparency and accountability, and helps in leveraging the cumulative knowledge of the community for better functioning. In line with this, PMKVY assigns special importance to the involvement of the target beneficiaries through a defined mobilisation process. TPs shall conduct Kaushal and Rozgar Melas every 6 months with press/media coverage. They are also required to participate actively in National Career Service Melas and on-ground activities.

11.10.4 Placement Guidelines: PMKVY envisages to link the aptitude, aspiration, and knowledge of the skilled workforce it creates with employment opportunities and demands in the

172   National Education Policy (NEP), 2020 and the Role of Teachers

market. Every effort thereby needs to be made by the PMKVY TCs to provide placement opportunities to candidates, trained and certified under the Scheme. TPs shall also provide support to entrepreneurship development.

11.10.5 Monitoring Guidelines: To ensure that high standards of quality are maintained by TCs, NSDC and empanelled inspection agencies shall use various methodologies, such as self-audit reporting, call validations, surprise visits, and monitoring through the Skills Development Management System (SDMS). These methodologies shall be enhanced with the engagement of latest technologies.

The scheme will be implemented through the National Skill Development Corporation (NSDC).

11.11 National Apprenticeship Training Scheme (NATS)

Apprenticeship is a time-tested way of learning a craft or trade under a master craftsman. Apprenticeship training is a procedure where young, technically qualified people undergo training under a master trainer to become equipped for jobs in the modern scenario. It has the double benefit of earning while learning. Apprenticeship is an agreement between a person (an apprentice) who wants to learn a skill and an employer who needs a skilled worker. The apprentices are taught the latest applications, processes and methodologies in their respective fields of work from some of the most renowned organisations in India. This also acts as a transition phase for a school/ college student from classroom to a working background. The apprentice also learns soft skills, work culture, ethics and organisational behaviour while undergoing training. This goes a long way in helping him/her secure permanent employment in the future. At the end of training they are issued a certificate attesting to their training and proficiency in a particular field. This serves as an experience certificate when they seek employment after their training.

NATS, sponsored by Ministry of Human Resource Development, Government of India, is a one year programme equipping technically qualified youth with practical knowledge and skills required in their field of work. The apprentices are imparted training by the organizations at their place of work. Trained managers with well-developed training modules ensure that apprentices learn the job quickly and competently. During the period of apprenticeship, the apprentices are paid a stipend amount, 50 percent of which is reimbursable to the employer from Government of India. At the end of the training period the apprentices are issued a certificate of proficiency by Government of India which can be registered at all employment exchanges across India as valid employment experience. The apprentices are placed for training at Central, State and private organizations which have excellent training facilities. NATS is one of the flagship programmes of Government of India for skilling Indian youth.

Endnote

1. Government of India, Ministry of Skill Development and Entrepreneurship, *National Skill Development Mission: A Framework for Implementation*, 2015, p. 2.

12

Adult Education

Literacy is the most essential pre-requisite for individual empowerment. Adult literacy and further education of the literates is as vital an area as universal elementary education.

12.1 National Literacy Mission (NLM)

A new thrust was given to adult literacy in the National Policy on Education (NPE), 1986 and the Plan of Action 1992, which advocated a three-pronged strategy of adult education, elementary education and non-formal education to eradicate illiteracy.

NLM was launched on May 5, 1988 as a Technology Mission to impart functional literacy to non-literates in the country in the age group of 15-35 years in a time-bound manner. This age-group has been the focus of attention because they are in the productive and reproductive period of life. NLM was set up with an initial target to make 80 million persons literate by 1995, which was later enhanced to 100 million by 1997 and the revised target was to achieve a threshold level of 75 percent literacy by 2007.

12.2 Total Literacy Campaign (TLC)

TLC has been the principal strategy of NLM for eradication of illiteracy in the target group. These campaigns are area-specific, time-bound, volunteer-based, cost-effective and outcome-oriented. They are implemented by *Zila Saksharata Samities* and district level literacy societies.

Keeping pace with its endeavours, campaigns and programmes, NLM has strengthened and revitalized the States Literacy Missions which have been imparted greater autonomy. They now have the authority to plan, implement

Adult Education

and monitor literacy programmes and sanction continuing education programmes at the State level. The NLM has also come to recognize the great potential that NGOs have in furthering its programmes and schemes. Given the major role, NGOs are now allowed to receive funds from *Zila Sakshara Samities* and actually run continuing education centres. The *Jan Shikshan Sansthans* have expanded their outreach and are also catering to the rural segment by offering vocational training courses.

At present, 595 districts are covered under the TLC and continuing education programmes is being implemented in 328 districts. In addition, 221 *Jan Shikshan Sansthan* have been set up to provide vocational training to the neo-literates and backward sections of the society. There are 25 state resource centres established for providing academic and technical resource support for the literacy programmes.

NLM has accorded priority for the promotion of female literacy. According to 2001 Census, 47 districts in the country had female literacy rate below 30 percent. Most of these districts were concentrated in Bihar, Jharkhand, Uttar Pradesh and Orissa. Special innovative projects have been taken up to raise the level of female literacy in these areas. Special efforts have been made to target female panchayati raj functionaries and make them literate.

12.3 *Jan Shikshan Sansthan* (JSS)

The objective of JSS scheme is educational, vocational and occupational development of socio-economically backward and educationally disadvantaged groups of urban/rural population, particularly neo-literates, semi-literates, scheduled castes, scheduled tribes, women and girls, slum dwellers, migrant workers etc. By linking literacy with vocational training, JSSs seek to improve the quality of life of the beneficiaries. JSSs offer around 284 different types of vocational courses—from candle and *agarbatti* making to computer training and hospital/healthcare. The total number of JSS is 221.

12.4 Saakshar Bharat

In the context of the Government's overall policy aimed at empowerment of women and in recognition of the fact that literacy is a prerequisite for socioeconomic development, the National Literacy Mission (NLM) has been recast as Saakshar Bharat, with prime focus on female literacy. This flagship programme of the Government covers all adults in the age group of 15 and above though its primary focus will be on women. Several new features have been added to the scheme and basic literacy, post-literacy, and continuing education programmes now form a continuum, rather than sequential segments under this programme. Besides, the volunteer-based mass campaign approach, provision has been made for alternative approaches to adult education. Jan Shiksha Kendras have been set up to co-ordinate and manage all programmes within their territorial jurisdiction. The State Governments, as against the districts in the earlier versions, and Panchyati Raj institutions, along with communities, are now the valued stakeholders. The budgetary support has also been substantially enhanced.

The focus of Saakshar Bharat is female literacy. While only 73 percent literacy has been achieved as per Census 2011, there is marked improvement in female literacy. Male literacy at 80.89 percent is still higher than female literacy at 64.64 percent but the latter increased by 10.9 percentage points compared to the 5.6 percentage points for the former. In recognition and appreciation of the programme's endeavour to establish a fully literate society, Saakshar Bharat was awarded the King Sejong Literacy Prize 2013 by the United Nations Educational, Scientific and Cultural Organization (UNESCO).

12.5 Weaknesses of Adult Education Programmes

The constraints in the implementation of adult education programmes include inadequate participation of the State Governments, low motivation and training of voluntary teachers/*preraks*, lack of convergence of programmes, and weak

Adult Education   177

management and supervision structure for implementation of NLM. Besides, the funding for various components of NLM schemes is inadequate and the level of community participation is also low.

While designing this programme, the lot of the weaker sections like women, scheduled castes, scheduled tribes and agricultural labourers as well as slum dwellers should be given priority. The strategy in these cases should be the development of methods and contents suited to the varied needs and situations, thus promoting flexibility in the means of delivery of education.

More intensive efforts are required to spread literacy in the rural and tribal areas which are lagging behind, with special attention to women and such marginalised groups as small and marginal farmers, landless labourers and educationally neglected tribal groups. For this purpose, a disaggregated and decentralised mode of planning and implementation should be adopted. Inter-linkage of the adult education programme with income generation, better health and nutrition, women's empowerment and overall rural development should be focussed upon. At the grassroots level, people's participation should be ensured in planning and implementation of local programmes.

12.6 Twelfth Five Year Plan (2012-17) on Adult Education

According to Twelfth Plan, "...there is a need to redefine literacy and go for a paradigm shift from basic literacy to lifelong learning. In the present technology-driven knowledge-based competitive economy, even the basic ability to read and write with understanding is not enough; adults need to learn to manage information and knowledge in a critical and reasonable manner, learn to search, identify, evaluate, select, and use information and knowledge wherever they are available: print, mass media, or the Internet. Nevertheless, becoming literate can no longer be viewed as a specific and terminal period in the life of a person. In fact, literacy is the entry point to basic education and a stepping stone to lifelong education. Lifelong learning is today essential for survival and for enhancing people's quality of life, as well as for national, human, social and economic development. It should cover 'all learning activity undertaken throughout life-whether in formal, non-formal and informal settings with the aim of improving knowledge, skills and competence within personal, civic, social and for employment related perspective'. Under this new paradigm of lifelong learning and literacy, the focus is not only on non-formal education set up but on establishing strong linkages with the formal system with mechanism for recognising prior learning and accreditation.

Accordingly, *Saakshar Bharat* would be revamped during the Twelfth Plan and aligned to the new paradigm of lifelong learning. The key features of this programme would be:

1. It would provide opportunities to meet all types of learning needs including functional literacy, basic education, vocational education, physical and emotional development, arts, culture, sports and recreation. Such opportunities of learning will be for all adults, disadvantaged and advantaged, in the age group of 15 years and above, who missed the opportunity of formal education as well as all adults who wish to learn outside the formal system of education. It would continue to focus on inclusion with programmatic interventions in rural areas, urban slums, low literacy areas, tribal areas, SCs and minority concentrated areas. To facilitate more equitable access and participation, the revamped programme would create appropriate infrastructure, especially in difficult, backward, tribal, and rural areas, and enhance culture of learning and education by eliminating barriers to participation through ICT, awareness, mobilisation, environment building and well-designed and targeted guidance, information and motivation.

2. At the Gram Panchayat level and at the equivalent levels in the urban areas, the existing well-equipped ICT-enabled multi-purpose adult education and skill development

Adult Education   179

centres (AESDCs) would be strengthened (or set up where these do not exist) to offer a range of adult learning and education programmes to meet local needs of the adults. For higher levels of adult education, secondary level institutions at the block and community colleges at the district level need to be set up.

3. Existing programme structures, including National Literacy Mission Authority at the apex level, the State Literacy Mission Authorities at the State level and the Lok Shiksha Samitis at the district, block and the gram panchayat, as well as the resource support bodies, would be remodelled, strengthened and aligned to lifelong learning and literacy. Inter-sectoral and inter-ministerial co-operation would be obtained. In addition, active involvement of public authorities at all administrative levels, civil society, private sector, community and adult learners' organisations in the development, implementation and evaluation of adult learning and education programmes would be obtained. The revamped programme would need a permanent system with nationwide and multilevel network of institutions and structures that conform to these parameters. Additional resources should be allocated for building capacities of PRIs and other implementing agencies.

4. Objective criteria to assess learning outcomes, skill development, prior learning and equivalency should be developed based on which third party assessment and certification should be undertaken. For this, partnerships should be developed with accredited national and State-level agencies and open and distance learning systems. *Lifelong learning and literacy* under the revamped programme should be seamlessly integrated with formal education system for horizontal and vertical migration by establishing equivalency frameworks to facilitate credit transfer among formal, non-formal and informal education.

The revamped *Saakshar Bharat* would be a continuing programme as a lifelong learning and literacy support system for the country. To promote a systematic lifelong learning, the country might require comprehensive legislation to formally recognize forms of education other than formal, integrate formal, non-formal and informal learning and for recognition, validation and accreditation of learning obtained in non-formal ways. Need for enabling legislative measures would thus be examined to provide a robust framework for lifelong learning and literacy". [1]

12.7 National Education Policy (NEP), 2020 on Adult Education and Lifelong Learning

According to NEP, 2020, "The opportunity to attain foundational literacy, obtain an education, and pursue a livelihood must be viewed as basic rights of every citizen. Literacy and basic education open up whole new worlds of personal, civic, economic, and lifelong-learning opportunities for individuals that enable them to progress personally and professionally. At the level of society and the nation, literacy and basic education are powerful force multipliers which greatly enhance the success of all other developmental efforts. Worldwide data on nations indicate extremely high correlations between literacy rates and per capita GDP.

Meanwhile, being a non-literate member of a community, has innumerable disadvantages, including the inability to: carry out basic financial transactions; compare the quality/quantity of goods purchased against the price charged; fill out forms to apply for jobs, loans, services, etc.; comprehend public circulars and articles in the news media; use conventional and electronic mail to communicate and conduct business; make use of the internet and other technology to improve one's life and profession; comprehend directions and safety directives on the street, on medicines, etc.; help children with their education; be aware of one 's basic rights and responsibilities as a citizen of India; appreciate works of literature; and pursue employment in medium or high-productivity sectors that require literacy. The abilities

Adult Education 181

listed here are an illustrative list of outcomes to be achieved through adoption of innovative measures for Adult Education.

Extensive field studies and analyses, both in India and across the world, clearly demonstrate that volunteerism and community involvement and mobilization are key success factors of adult literacy programmes, in conjunction with political will, organizational structure, proper planning, adequate financial support, and high-quality capacity building of educators and volunteers. Successful literacy programmes result not only in the growth of literacy among adults, but also result in increased demand for education for all children in the community, as well as greater community contribution to positive social change. The National Literacy Mission, when it was launched in 1988, was largely based on the voluntary involvement and support of the people, and resulted in significant increases in national literacy during the period of 1991-2011, including among women, and also initiated dialogue and discussions on pertinent social issues of the day. Strong and innovative government initiatives for adult education—in particular, to facilitate community involvement and the smooth and beneficial integration of technology—will be affected as soon as possible to expedite this all-important aim of achieving 100 percent literacy". [2]

Endnotes

1. Government of India, Planning Commission, *Twelfth Five Year Plan (2012-17)*, Volume III, Chapter 21, paras 21.177 to 21.179.
2. Government of India, Ministry of Human Resource Development, *National Education Policy 2020*, p. 51.

13

Internet and Education

Internet is a vast and connected network of individual computers and computer networks for the purpose of communicating with each other, using the same communication protocol—Transmission Control Protocol/Internet Protocol (TCP/IP). When two or more computers are connected a network is created. When two or more networks are connected, an *internetwork* (or internet) is created. The internet, as commonly understood, is the largest example of such a system. Internet is often and aptly described as *Information Superhighway*, a means to reach innumerable potential destinations. The destination can be any one of the connected networks and host computers.

13.1 Major Uses of Internet

These are the following:

13.1.1 File Transfer Protocol (FTP): It is a mechanism for transferring files between computers on the internet. It is possible to transfer a file to and from a computer (FTP site) without having an account in that machine. Any organization intending to make available to public its documents would normally set up a FTP site from which any one can access the documents for download. Certain FTP sites are available to validated users with an account ID and password.

13.1.2 Electronic-mail (E-mail): The most common and basic use of internet is the exchange of e-mail. It is an extremely powerful and revolutionary result of internet which has facilitated almost instantaneous communication with people in any part of the world. With enhancements like attachment of documents, audio, video and voice mail, this segment of internet is fast expanding as the most used communication medium for the whole world. Many websites offer e-mail as a free facility to individuals. Many corporates have interfaced their private networks with internet in order to make their e-mail accessible from outside their corporate network.

13.1.3 World Wide Web (WWW): Internet encompasses any electronic communication between computers using TCP/IP protocol, such as e-mail, file transfers etc. WWW is a segment of nternet, which uses Hyper Text Mark-up Language (HTML) to link together files containing text, rich text, sound, graphics, video etc. and offers a very convenient means of navigating through the net. It uses hypertext transfer protocol (HTTP) for communication between computers. Web documents, which are referred to as pages, can contain links to other related documents in a tree like structure.

The person browsing one document can access any other linked page. The web documents and the web browsers which are the application programmes to access them, are designed to be platform independent. Thus, any web document can be accessed irrespective of the platform of the computer accessing the document and that of the host computer. The *point and click* method of browsing is extremely simple for any lay user of the net. In fact, the introduction of web since early 1990 has made internet an extremely popular medium and its use in business has been enhanced dramatically.

The next in the HTML genre is the Extensible Mark-up Language (XML), which allows automated two-way information flow between data stores and browser screens. XML documents provide both the raw content of data and the data structure and are projected by its proponents as taking the web technology beyond the limits of HTML.

13.1.4 Wireless Application Protocol (WAP): WAP is the latest industry standard which provides wireless access to internet through hand-held devices like a cellular telephone. This is an open standard promoted by WAP forum and has been adopted by all major handset manufacturers of the world. WAP is supplemented by Wireless Application Environment

(WAE), which provides industry-wise standard for developing applications and services for wireless communication networks. This is based on WWW technology and provides for application for small screens, with interactive capabilities and adequate security. Wireless Transaction Protocol (WTP), which is the equivalent of TCP, sets the communication rules and Wireless Transport Layer Security (WTLS) provides the required security by encrypting all the session data. WAP is set to revolutionize the commercial use of net.

13.2 Internet and Students

It is recognized that the use of internet for educational purposes has been growing rapidly as internet assignments and internet-mediated instruction replace face-to-face class time. Internet has been helpful in containing the rising costs of higher education, accommodates more diverse body of students and may also be effective than courses that are delivered face-to-face. There are three functions of computer enhanced instruction model—information, instruction and communication—that aim at increasing student participation, enhancing written communication skills and focusing the learning experience on interaction and reflection.

Internet has resulted in two major advantages for students. First, it offers a new medium of interaction that complements classroom instruction and facilitates learning. Second, it offers the opportunity to learn, use internet technology and yield positive externalities for future academic and career paths.

Internet can improve the productivity and efficiencies of university academicians as they can use internet to improve their skills and get any knowledge and information.

The main goal of acceptance of rapid developments in technology by the education sector is to support learning and teaching to make the best schools, teachers, and courses available to all students without regard to gender, distance, resources, or disabilities, i.e. teaching without discrimination.

The wealth of information on internet is growing

Internet and Education

exponentially each day and has replaced the dominant sources or vehicle of knowledge, i.e. books and papers. Utilizing these traditional ways of obtaining information was a tedious job when it came down to searching for a specific piece of information through the index or table of contents. In addition to this, the information was confined to the pages of a book, which became a handicap, as information must always be updated and available on demand at immediate basis. Internet has not just rendered these sources of information as un-economical in terms of time, costs and space, but also equipped users with multi-media and hyper-linking capabilities that allow information to be presented in the form of sounds, videos and pictures with no limit on number of users who could use it simultaneously.

Internet breaks the boundary of traditional classroom by allowing teachers and pupils to have immediate connection to the outside world.

Students find value in electronic communication as it provides better access to instructor, more interesting assignments and advocate future use of e-mail in their academic and professional careers. The greater interaction between the instructors and the students and hands-on learning of new concepts are results of effectiveness of internet usage.

Computer-enhanced format of instruction is marked more favourable for helpfulness of discussions with other students, ease-of-contact with the instructor, and opportunities for expressing and sharing ideas. Instructors rely on internet to provide course material, direct assignments and readings, and obtain feedback from students, whereas students can read, process, and analyze information, discuss the issues with their peers, and complete assignments.

Academicians are able to communicate with their worldwide colleagues through internet and discussion groups allow users to follow issues of interest and keep themselves up-to-date on these issues. It also serves as a tool for supporting networking among professionals in different geographical locations.

Computer conferencing allows for increased interaction and discussion, which results in increased ability of students to apply theory and thus stimulate their perceptions and interests towards their subjects.

13.3 Collaborative Teaching

Nothing in history has been as powerful as the internet in terms of changing traditional roles of teacher as an expert and student as passive receptacle for handover of knowledge. Active and expression learning has shifted traditional information-giving to pupil's participation in information-gathering, interpretation and use. Internet is like a vehicle for teachers to create high performance learning environments through which the goals of the various dimensions of schooling can be accomplished.

Through resources available via the internet, students may be provided opportunities to engage in authentic, challenging activities. Teachers can set meaningful, challenging activities as the centre of instruction. Classroom approaches that support such a paradigm might include collaborative learning, heterogeneous groupings, teacher as facilitator, performance-based assessment, peer-to-peer mentoring, multi-disciplinary curriculum, interactive modes of instruction, student exploration, and extended blocks of time.

Computer communication and ease of information retrieval through the internet allow higher development of critical thinking and problem solving, foster independence and autonomy, and permit greater interaction. Moreover, better correspondence fosters thought and interest in the subject matter and hands-on experience makes understanding and learning process more active.

Web technology has shifted the ability to control information flow from the information provider to the users. Moreover, pupils can now acquire their own communication links for exploring topics beyond the boundaries of the traditional concept of school and they can quickly access

Internet and Education

learning resources at any hour of the day while studying at home, or in a library or any place with internet connection.

In the education sector also, MOOCs (Massive Open Online Courses) have been successfully implemented by the top universities of the world because of the availability of internet services.

13.4 Newspaper Reading

The three key elements that drive the newspaper industry are content, delivery and advertising, which internet is very well capable of providing at much lesser costs. In addition to this, it also provides convenience of reading news as per discretion and availability of time—cost advantages for those who have free internet access and allows for simultaneous scanning of two-three similar news-sites to find out the view different opinions on the same issue.

Also, the amount of information available is abundant and easily accessible from anywhere. Internet has resulted in time displacement of newspapers and is more popular in case of business/stock news, sport news and international news. Reading news on internet is complimentary to reading newspaper and it is not substituting newspaper.

13.5 Internet for Research and Academics

13.5.1 Worldwide Connectivity: Internet is a global network of networks which connect more number of people each day in different countries worldwide to millions of computers. Internet creates an environment in which information is shared with colleagues in cross-disciplinary research that spans across the globe. Internet fosters the creation of virtual communities of individuals who are geographically distant but linked with common interests and concerns.

Internet provides information originating from governments, institutions, corporations, or individuals for a wide array of purposes that include research, learning, business, politics, charity and leisure in various forms like e-mail, web pages, blogs, wiki

188 National Education Policy (NEP), 2020 and the Role of Teachers

resources, instant messages, open access journals and books. It is for these reasons, that users consider it as the first choice for information search.

Internet has an ability to store billions of records such as complex data sets, high-resolution graphics, sounds, videos and animation that are available in addition to plentiful databases and documents.

Complete accessibility of educational resources via the internet generates consequences in relation to knowledge creation and raises concerns as to whether the timeframes traditionally associated with research degrees should be reduced in acknowledgement of benefits that arise out of more proficient information retrieval and efficient effects of word processing on academic writing. This development of technology has resulted in reduction of social complexity that is innate in traditional system of interaction and has maximized benefits for academics.

Internet provides a coherent view of a library of files that are distributed across host computers all over the world. In addition to this, hyper-linking has also allowed them to follow the thread of one file on one computer to a related file on another and thus creates an increased demand for means of information search.

Internet is a very useful reference tool as it includes documents in different media, both hardcopy and electronic, besides to non-conventional sources of information such as information centres, individual experts and electronic mailing lists. Internet has the ability to answer wide range of questions and is a stable reference medium as internet-based results can be verified with a traditional reference source. Many research professionals use it as an instrument of choice rather than a tool of last resort.

Interactive nature of the internet plays a formative role in the discussion of original results or findings and provides a venue in which scholars from around the world can participate in the reasoning and sculpt the information into a larger and cohesive

Internet and Education

whole. Internet has the ability to support collaborative research and writing as it facilitates exchange and modification of textual material by writers who can interact through a range of software types and makes assembling of electronic textual material a reality.

13.5.2 Plagiarism and Copyright Issues: The ready availability of massive amounts of material in useable form significantly facilitates the problem of plagiarism. It gives rise to copyright issues as it seeks the prior consent of original author/owner of electronically mediated textual information.

Internet age has given rise to issues of copyright, freedom of access to information and enfranchisement. Research information on the web comes with varying quality, as some information is available without any name or affiliation, which is a major determinant of reliability of information.

13.5.3 Virtual Library: Virtual libraries are libraries without walls and internet provides the windows and transparency to these libraries. It allows users that are physically isolated from the library to see in and those who are inside the library to see out. Internet plays an inevitable role in virtual libraries as they have become of core importance for distance learning programmes. The widespread access of internet into homes of students ensures the success of these schemes and facilitates the libraries to offer course materials and other documents electronically to students scattered over wide areas, particularly rural areas.

Just as libraries are getting transformed into databases of digital objects from being brick-and-mortar structures, librarians are also getting transitioned from being custodian of books to being leaders and enablers of the information. The librarian needs to be a teacher of and guide to the resources available, and also an advocate to ensure that these resources continue to be available and new ones are continually brought forward.

13.6 Negative Aspects

The entire schooling system needs to be re-engineered in

190 National Education Policy (NEP), 2020 and the Role of Teachers

the era of internet, where students are more detached from a single school and the teachers therein and open to more opportunities of interacting directly with other schools and *knowledge providers* on the internet. On top of this, web technology has made both publishing and retrieval of information accessible to many, due to which schools will now have to be gatekeepers in short-listing books and educational websites that students can read and visit as finding relevant information becomes difficult in such a loosely-controlled and independent environment. Internet is anarchic in a way that it is accessible by anyone anywhere in the world and anyone anywhere can publish anything. Without proper management, the internet could become a potential threat to the well-being of a school and its pupils when they are internet connected.

13.7 National Education Policy (NEP), 2020 on Online and Digital Education

According to NEP, 2020, "New circumstances and realities require new initiatives. The recent rise in epidemics and pandemics necessitates that we are ready with alternative modes of quality education whenever and wherever traditional and in-person modes of education are not possible. In this regard, the National Education Policy 2020 recognizes the importance of leveraging the advantages of technology while acknowledging its potential risks and dangers. It calls for carefully designed and appropriately scaled pilot studies to determine how the benefits of online/digital education can be reaped while addressing or mitigating the downsides. In the meantime, the existing digital platforms and ongoing ICT-based educational initiatives must be optimized and expanded to meet the current and future challenges in providing quality education for all.

However, the benefits of online/digital education cannot be leveraged unless the digital divide is eliminated through concerted efforts, such as the Digital India campaign and the availability of affordable computing devices. It is important

Internet and Education

that the use of technology for online and digital education adequately addresses concerns of equity.

Teachers require suitable training and development to be effective online educators. It cannot be assumed that a good teacher in a traditional classroom will automatically be a good teacher in an online classroom. Aside from changes required in pedagogy, online assessments also require a different approach. There are numerous challenges to conducting online examinations at scale, including limitations on the types of questions that can be asked in an online environment, handling network and power disruptions, and preventing unethical practices. Certain types of courses/subjects, such as performing arts and science practical have limitations in the online/digital education space, which can be overcome to a partial extent with innovative measures. Further, unless online education is blended with experiential and activity-based learning, it will tend to become a screen-based education with limited focus on the social, affective and psychomotor dimensions of learning". [1]

Endnote

1. Government of India, Ministry of Human Resource Development, *National Education Policy 2020*, pp. 58-59.

Bibliography

Bibliography

Agarwal, J.C. (1994), "Essentials of Educational Psychology", New Delhi: Vikas Publishing House.

Agarwal, M. (1985), "Essentials of Educational Psychology", New Delhi: Vikas Publishing House.

Aggarwal, Y.P. (2002), "Statistical Methods: Concepts, Application and Computation", New Delhi: Sterling Publishers.

Agnes, Ebi Maliki (2013), "Attitudes towards the Teaching Profession of Students from Faculty of Education", Niger Delta University, *International Journal of Social Science Research*, Vol. 1, Issue 1, pp. 11-18.

Ahluwalia, S.P. (1978), "A Study of Change in Professional Attitude of Student Teachers", *Journal of Institute of Educational Research*, 2(1), pp. 26-34.

Akbulut and Karakus (2011), "The Investigation of Secondary School Science and Mathematics Pre-service Teachers' Attitudes towards Teaching Profession", *Educational Research and Reviews*, 6(6), pp. 489-496, available at: http://www.academicjournals.org/ERR.

Akkaya, F. (2009), "Pre-service Teacher's Attitude towards the Teaching Profession", Inonu University, *Journal of the Faculty of Education*, 9(6), pp. 27-42.

Alharbi, Asma, Mohammed (2013), "Teacher's Attitudes towards Integrating Technology: Case Studies in Saudi Arabia and the United States", Masters Theses, Paper 58.

Anastasi, A. (1990), "Psychological Testing", New York: Macmillan Publishing Company.

Anderson-DeWayne, B. and Anderson-Ariel, L.H. (1995), "Pre-service Teachers' Attitudes towards Children: Implications for Teacher Education", *Educational Forum*, 59(3), pp. 312-318.

Arora, K. and Chopra, B. (1969), "A Study of Status of Teacher Educators working in Elementary Teacher Training Institutions", Department of Teacher Education, NCERT, New Delhi.

Ashton, P.T. and Webb, R.B. (1986), "Making a Difference: Teacher's Sense of Efficacy and Student Achievement", New York: Longman.

Austin, A.N. (1985), "A Study of the Attitudes of Teachers and Principals towards Mainstreaming Practices at Selected Elementary Schools in the District of Columbia", International Dissertation Abstracts, 45, 8, 2315-A.

Austin, G.G. (1979), "The Effects of Student Teaching and Pre-Testing on Student Teacher's Attitude", *Journal of Experimental Education*, 48, pp. 36-38.

Badola, Sunitha (2010), "A Study of IGNOU (B.Ed Teacher Trainees Attitude towards Awareness of the Fundamental Rights of Secondary Students", *Vivek Journal of Education and Research*, 1(3), pp. 25-27.

Baer, J. (1997), "Creative Teachers, Creative Students", Boston: Allen and Bacon.

Balan, K. (1996), "Attitude towards Teaching Profession and Self-Concept of Student Teachers of Kerala", unpublished M.Ed. Dissertation, University of Calicut.

Ball, S.J. and Goodson, I.F. (1985), "Teachers' Lives and Careers", London: Falmer Press.

Banerjee, Srijita and Santosh Kumar Behera (2014), "An Investigation into the Attitude of Secondary School Teachers towards Teaching Profession in Purulia District of West Bengal, India", *Academic Research Journal*, 2(3), pp. 56-63.

Baxter, Anthony G. (1993), "Improving Teaching Candidates Attitude towards learning Theoretical Knowledge: Seeking Change in Teacher Education and Practice", 8(2), pp. 15-25.

Belagali, H.V. (2011), "A Study of Teachers Attitude towards Teaching Profession of Secondary Schools in Relation to Gender and Locality", *International Referred Research Journal*, III (32), pp. 18-19.

Bem, D.J. (1970), "Beliefs, Attitudes, and Human Affairs", California: Wadsworth Publishing Co.

Best, John, W. (1963), "Research in Education" New Delhi: Prentice Hall of India Pvt. Ltd.

Bhargava, Anupma and Pathy, M.K. (2014), "Attitude of Students Teacher towards Teaching", *Turkish Online Journal of Distance Education*, 15.

Bhandarkar, B.G. (1980), "A Study of a Polytechnic Teacher's Attitude towards Teaching Profession and its Correlates", Government Polytechnic, Jalgaon.

Bozdogan, A.E., Aydin, D. and Yildirin, K. (2007), "Teacher's

Bibliography 197

Attitude towards Teaching Profession", *Kireehir Journal of Education*, 8(2), pp. 83-97.

Budhisagar, Meena and Samsanwal, D.N. (1991), "Achievement of B.Ed. Students: Effect of Treatment, Intelligence, Attitude towards Teaching Profession and their Interactions", Fifth Survey of Research in Education, New Delhi: NCERT, 1440.

Bullemma, M. (2010), "Interpersonal Relationship of Prospective Teachers", M.Ed dissertation, Acharya Nagarjuna University.

Bloom, B.S., Hatings, J.T. and Madaus, C.E. (1971), "Handbook on Formative and Summative Evaluation of Student Learning", New York: McGraw Hill Co.

Buch, M.B. (1983), "Third Survey of Research in Education (1978-83)", Baroda: M.S. University.

Buch, M.B. (1988), "Fourth Survey of Research in Education (1983-88)", New Delhi: NCERT.

Cantril, H. (1965), "The Pattern of Human Concern", New Brunswick, NJ: Rutgers University Press.

Capa, Y. and Cil, N. (2000), "Teacher's Attitude towards Teaching Profession: An Investigation of the Different Variables", *Hacettepe University Journal of Education*, 18, pp. 69-73.

Carlson, E.R. (1956), "Attitude Change through Modification of Attitude Structure", *Journal of Abnormal and Social Psychology*, 52, pp. 256-261.

Celikoz, N. and Cetin, F. (2004), "Anatohan Teacher High School Students' Attitude about the Factors Affecting the Teaching Profession", *National Education Journal*, 162, pp. 234-241.

Charalambous, C. Panaoura, A. and Philippou, G. (2009), "Using the History of Mathematics to Induce Changes in Pre-service Teachers' Beliefs and Attitudes: Insights from Evaluating a Teacher Education Program", *Educational Studies in Mathematics*, 71(2), pp. 161-180.

Chidolu, Mercy, E. (1996), "The Relationship between Teacher Characteristics, Learning Environment and Student Achievement and Attitude", *Studies in Educational Evaluation*, 22(3), pp. 263-274.

Clifford, S. Zimmerman (1999), "Thinking Beyond my Own Interpretations: Reflections on Collaborative and Cooperative Learning Theory in the Law School Curriculum", 31 ARIZ. ST. L.J. 957.

Cornelius (2000), "Teacher Competence Associated with

Intelligence, Attitude towards Teaching Profession and Academic Achievement of Teacher Trainees", unpublished M.Phil Thesis, University of Kerala.

Creswell, John, W. (2003), "Research Design: Qualitative, Quantitative and Mixed Method Approaches", Thousand Oaks, California: Sage Publications.

Deas, Alberta, D. (1978), "Performance-based Vocational Teacher Education: An Assessment of Attitudes of Teacher Trainees and Teacher Educators at Westfield State College", dissertation, *Abstract International*, 39.

Devi, Usha, V.K. (2005), "A Study of Role Conflict, Job Satisfaction and Select Presage Variables Discriminating between Successful and Less Successful Secondary School Women Teachers of Kerala", doctoral thesis, University of Calicut.

Donald, A.O. (2009), "Secondary Students Attitude towards the Teaching", *Education Community*, USA.

Downing, Jan E., Filer, Janet D. and Chamberlain, Robert A. (1997), "Science Process Skills and Attitudes of Pre-service Elementary Teachers", *Reports Research*, 143.

Dwivedi, Shri Kant (2012), "Impact of Pre-service Teacher Education on Teaching Competence, Teaching Aptitude and Attitude towards Teaching", Ph.D. thesis, IASE, MJP Rohilkhand University, Bareilly.

Eagle, A. and Chaiken, S. (1993), "The Psychology of Attitude", ForthWorth, TX: Harcourt Brace Jovanovich.

Feldman D. (1985), "Handbook of Intellectual and Developmental Disabilities", p. 149.

Fishbein, H.D. (1967), "Peer Prejudice and Discrimination: The Origins or Prejudice", Hahwah, New Jersey, London: Lawrence Erlbaum Associates Publishers.

Freeman, Frank S. (1959), "Theory and Practice of Psychological Testing", p. 484.

Garret H.I. (1973), "Statistics in Psychology and Education", Bombay: Vikils Fefter & Simons Pvt. Ltd.

Gepi, A. (1981), "A Study of Relationship of Academic Achievement with Attitude towards Teaching among Teacher-Trainees", in Buch, M.B., "Third Survey of Research in Education", Baroda: Society for Educational Research and Development, 1978-1983, p. 804.

George, A. and Ferguson Y.T. (1970), "Statistical Analysis in

Bibliography   199

Psychology and Education", New York: McGraw Hill Book Company.

Gerald, Anderson (2009), "Achieving Teaching Excellence: A Step-by-Step Guide", A1 Book Co.

Gill, T.K. and Saini, S.K. (2005), "Effect of Teacher Education on Attitude of Student Teachers towards the Teaching Profession", *Anveshika, Indian Journal of Teacher Education*, 2, pp. 8-14.

Good, C.V. (1959), "Dictionary of Education", New York: McGraw Hill Co. Inc.

Goodwin, Deborah, P and Deering, Rose Marie J. (1993), "The Interactive Video Approach to Pre-service Teacher Training: An Analysis of Students'' Perceptions and Attitudes", *Teacher Education and Practice*, 9(1), pp. 11-19.

Government of India (1948-49), "Report of the University Educational Commission (1948-49)", New Delhi: Ministry of Education.

Government of India (1971), "Education and National Development (1964-66)", New Delhi: NCERT.

Government of India (1986), "National Policy on Education, 1986", New Delhi: Ministry of Human Resource Development.

Government of India (2020), "National Education Policy, 2020", New Delhi: Ministry of Human Resource Development.

Gregory J.P. and Russell W.R. (2008), "Teacher Effectiveness in First Grade: The Importance of Background Qualifications, Attitudes and Instructional Practices for Student Learning", *Journal of Educational Evaluation and Policy Analysis*, USA: Sage Publications, 30, (2), pp. 111-140.

Guilford (1954), "Psychometric Methods", New York: McGraw-Hill Book Company.

Gupta, A.K. (1984), "Teacher Education: Current Trends and Prospects", New York: Sterling Publishers.

Hogben, D. and Petty, M. (1979), "Early Changes in Teacher Attitude", *Educational Research*, pp. 212-219.

Hosgorur, V. Kilic, O. and Dundar, H. (2002), "Kirikale University Classroom Teaching Programme: Student's Attitudes towards the Teaching Profession", Marmara University, Faculty of Education, *Science Journal*, 8(16), pp. 91-100.

Huber, Tonya and Kline, Frank (1993), "Attitudes toward Diversity: Can Teacher Education Programs Really Make a Difference?", *Teacher Educator*, 29(1), pp. 15-23.

Hussain et al. (2011), "Relationship between the Professional Attitudes of Secondary School Teachers with their Teaching Behaviour", *International Journal of Academic Research in Business and Social Sciences,* 1(3), pp. 38-46.

Hussain, Shaukat (2004), "Effectiveness of Teacher Training in Developing Professional Attitude of Prospective Secondary School Teachers", Ph.D. thesis.

Jain, B. (1982), **"**A Study of Classroom Behaviour Patterns of Teachers in Relation to their Attitude towards Profession, Morale and Values", JMI, Third Survey of Research in Education, 1978-83, p. 763.

Jennings, L. (1980), "Educational and Psychological Measurement", 41, pp. 1167-1174.

Kanekar, S. (1989), "Attitude Formation and Change", Mumbai: Jaico Publishing House.

Karlinger, Fred N. (1973), "Foundation of Behavioural Research", New York: Sage Publications.

Karp-Karen-Silliman (1991), "Elementary School Teachers' Attitudes towards Mathematics, the Impact of Student's Autonomous Learning Skills", *School Science and Mathematics,* 91(6), pp. 265-70.

Kaul, L. (1984), "Methodology of Educational Research", New Delhi: Vikas Publishing House.

Kaur, Harvinder (2009), "Impact of B.Ed. Programme on Teacher Effectiveness, Personality, Teaching Aptitude and Attitude towards Teaching of Prospective Teachers", Ph.D. thesis, Chandigarh: Punjab University.

Kerlinger, N. (1984), "Foundations of Behavioural Research: Education and Psychological Inquiry", New York: Hit Ripehand.

Khatoon, Tahira (1985), "Relationship between Teacher's Classroom Verbal Behaviour and their Attitude towards Teaching", *Journal of the Institute of Educational Research.*

Kiesler, C.A. (1971), "Attitudes and Opinions", *Annual Review of Psychology,* 26, pp. 415-456.

Kottler, J.A. and Kottler, E. (2005), "Counselling Skills for Teachers", New York: Sage Publications.

Koul, Lokesh (1977), **"**A Study of the Impact of Teacher Training upon Attitude of Student Teachers towards Teaching", *Indian Educational Review,* 12, p. 38.

Bibliography 201

Krathwohl, David (1964), "Taxonomy of Educational Objectives Handbook 2", New York: David McKay.

Kretch, David and Crutchfield, Richard S. (1948), "Theory and Problems of Social Psychology", New York: McGraw-Hill Publication.

Kumar, Ajith, V.K. (1995), "A Study of Attitude of Teacher Trainees towards Teaching Profession", M.Ed. dissertation, University of Kerala.

Lacey, Colin (1977), "The Socialization of Teachers", London: Methuen and Co. Ltd.

Lacy et al. (1983), "The psychology of Inter-group Attitudes and Behaviour", *Annual Review of Psychology*.

Lasely, Thomas J. (1975), "Pre-service Teacher Beliefs about Teaching", *Journal of Teacher Education*, 31(4), p. 38.

Litt, M.D. and Turk, D.C. (1985), "Sources of Stress and Dissatisfaction in Experienced High School Teachers", *Journal of Educational Research*, 78, 3, pp. 178-185.

Lawal, B.O. (2012), "Analysis of Parents, Teachers, and Students' Perception of Teaching Profession in Southwest Nigeria", *Asian Social Science*, 8(1), pp. 119-124.

Lortie, D. (1975), "Schoolteacher: A Sociological Study", London: University of Chicago Press.

Mahapatra, P.L. (1987), "Comparative Role of Intelligence, Attitude and Vocational Interest towards Success in Teaching", doctoral thesis, Utkal University.

Mangal, S.K. (2007), "Psychology of Teaching and Learning", Meerut: Loyal Publications.

Marete, Elizabeth Cirindi (2004), "A Study of Teachers' Attitudes towards the Implementation of Free Primary Education in Public Primary Schools in Kikuyu Division", research project, University of Nairobi.

Marso, Ronald. N., Pigge, Fred, L. (1996), "Relationship between Pre- and Post-preparation Development of Attitudes, Anxieties and Confidence about Teaching and Candidate's Success or Failure in Making the Transition to Teaching", paper presented at the annual Meeting of the Mid Western Educational Research Association, Chicago, IL, October 25.

Mathai, M. (1992), "Some Presage Variables Discriminating between Successful and Less Successful Secondary School Science Teachers of Kerala", M.Phil. thesis, University of

Calicut.

Mehrotra, R.N. (1973), "Effect of Teacher Education Programmes on the Attitude of Teachers towards the Teaching Profession", CIE, Delhi, Ph.D. survey of Research in Education, p. 438.

Mohammad, Iqbal Mattoo and Tariq Abdullah, Bichoo (2014), "Attitude of Secondary School Teachers towards Teaching with Special Reference to Rural and Urban Background", *Indian Journal of Research*, 3, p. 2.

Mohsin, S.M. (1990), "Attitude: Concept, Formation and Change", New Delhi: Wiley Eastern Publications.

Nuri Baloglu & Engin, Karadag (2008), "A Study of the Relationship between the Prospective Teachers Attitudes towards the Teaching Profession and their Preferred Coping Strategies with Stress", available at:
http://www.educationalrev.us.edu.pl /e19/a21.pdf.

Oskamp, S. (1977), "Attitudes and Opinions", Hahwah, New Jersey, London: Lawrence Erlbaum Associates Publishers.

Osunde, A.U. and Izevbigie, T.I. (2006), "An Assessment of Teachers Attitude towards Teaching Profession in Midwestern Nigeria", *Education,* 126(3), pp. 462-467.

Pandey, K.P. (1988), "Advanced Educational Psychology", New Delhi: Konark Publishers Pvt. Ltd.

Pedersen, J.E. and McCurdy, D.W. (1992), "The Effects on Hands-on Minds-on Teaching Experience on Attitudes of Pre-service Elementary Teachers", *Science Education*, 76(2), pp. 141-146.

Piel, John A. and Green, Michael (1992), "Educational Attitudes of Pre-service Teachers or Redesigning the Excel of Teacher Education".

Pigge, Fred L. and Marso, Ronald, N. (1997), "Development of Attitude towards Teaching Career in a Longitudinal Sample of Teacher Candidates Progressing through Preparation and Five Years of Teaching".

Poozhikuth, M. (1989), "Attitude towards Teaching Profession of College Teachers", M.Ed dissertation, University of Calicut.

Pugh, Ava F. and Others (1991), "An investigation of Pre-service Teacher's Attitudes towards Theory and Practical Application in Teacher Preparation".

Pushpam, A.M. (2003), "Attitude towards Teaching Profession and Job Satisfaction of Women Teachers in Coimbatore", *Journal of Educational Research and Extension*, 1, 40(2), Coimbatore.

Bibliography

Quinn, R. (1997), "Effects of Mathematics Methods Courses on the Mathematical Attitudes and Content Knowledge of Pre-service Teachers", *The Journal of Educational Research*, 91(2), pp. 108-119.

Ramakrishnaih, D. (1989), "Job Satisfaction of College Teachers", doctoral thesis, Sri Venkateswara University.

Ramakrishnanaih, D. (1980), "A Study of Job Satisfaction, Attitude towards Teaching and Job Involvement of College Teachers", M.Phil dissertation, Sri Venkateswara University.

Rawat, S. and Srivastava, R.K. (1984), "Attitude of Male and Female Teacher Trainees towards Teaching: A Comparative Study", *Asian Journal of Psychology and Education*, 13, pp. 54-58.

Rao, R.B. (1986), "A Study of Inter-Relationship of Values, Adjustment and Teaching Attitude of Pupil-Teachers at Various Levels of Socio-economic Status", in Buch. M.B., Fourth Survey (1983-1988) of Research in Education, Baroda Society for Educational Research and Development, II, p. 980.

Reddy, K.B. (1995), "A Study of Student Teachers' Success in Relation to Criteria of Admission and Attitude towards Teaching", *The Progress of Education*, Pune, LXX, pp. 12-14.

Rokeach, Milton (1960), "The Open and Closed Mind: Investigations into the Nature of Belief Systems and Personality Systems", New York: Basic Books, Inc.

Sahaya, Mary. R, and Samuel, Manorama (2011), "Relationship between Attitude of the B.Ed. Student-Teachers towards Teaching and Academic Achievement", *Edutracks*, Hyderabad: Neelkamal, 10, (6), pp. 28-35.

Santwana, Mishra, G. (2007), "Teaching Attitude Score: A Criterion for Admission in Colleges of Education", *Edutracks*, February, 6(6), pp. 25-27.

Selvaraj, Gnanagur A. and Suresh Kumar, M. (2008), "A Study of Under Achievement of B.Ed. Students in Relation to their Home Environment and Attitude towards Teaching", *Edutracks,* 7(12), pp. 20-22.

Sharbain and Tan (2013), "Gender Differences in Primary English Language Teachers' towards the Teaching Profession", *Wudpecker Journal of Educational Research*, 2(5), p. 071-077.

Sharma, Rekha (2013), "A Comparative Study of Teaching Competency, Attitude towards Teaching and Professional Commitment of BTC and special BTC Primary Teachers", Ph.D.

thesis, IASE, CCS University, Meerut.

Sharma, R.C. (1970), "To Investigate the Professional Needs of Teacher Educators of Undergraduate Training Institutions of Madhya Pradesh and Maharashtra", Survey of Research in Education, 1974, p. 463.

Singh, H.L. (1974), "Measurement of Teacher Values and their Relationships with Teacher Attitudes and job Satisfaction", D.Phil. (Education) BHU, Second Survey of Research in Education, p. 448.

Skariah, Sunny (1994), "Study of Creativity in Student Teachers in Relation to their Self-concept, Attitude towards Teaching and Success in Teaching", Ph.D thesis, Department of Education, University of Kerala.

Taiwo, D. (1980), "The Influence of Previous Exposure to Science Education on Attitudes of Pre-service Science Teacher towards Science Teaching", *Journal of Research in Science Teaching*, 17, pp. 84-89.

Tashakkori, A. and Teddlie, C. (1998), "Mixed Methodology: Combining Quantitative and Qualitative Approaches", Thousand Oaks,CA: Sage Publications.

Teddlie, Ch. (2005), Mixed Methods Research Tradition in English, F-(Ed.) Encyclopaedia of Educational Administration. Thousand Oaks, California: Sage Publications.

Theurer, J. (2006), "Tell Me What You Know; Pre-service Teachers Attitudes towards Teaching Comprehension", *The Reading Matrix*, 6, pp. 113-120.

Thurstone L.L. (1931), "The Measurement of Social Attitudes", *Journal of Abnormal and Social Psychology*, 27, pp. 249-269.

Tracy Darrin, Wood (2012), "Teacher Perceptions of Gender-Based Differences among Elementary School Teachers", *International Electronic Journal of Elementary Education*, 4(2), pp. 317-345.

Twillie, Less Doll and Others (1992), "Improving Academic Achievement in Inner City Schools: Do Attitudes of Parents and Teachers Make a Difference"?

Philippou, G. and Christou, C. (1998), "The Effects of a Preparatory Mathematics Program in Changing Prospective Teachers' Attitudes towards Mathematics", *Educational Studies in Mathematics*, 23(2), pp. 189-206.

Upadhyay, B. (1984), "A Comparative Study of the Attitude, Value and Motivation of the Pupil Teachers of Sampuranand Sanskrit

Bibliography

Viswa Vidyalaya and other Universities of Uttar Pradesh", in Buch, M.B., Fourth Survey of Research in Education, Baroda Society for Educational Research and Development, II, p. 1002.

Quinn, R. (1997), "Effects of Mathematics Methods Courses on the Mathematical Attitudes and Content knowledge of Pre-service Teachers", *The Journal of Educational Research*, 91(2), pp. 108-119.

Sweeting Kylie (2011), "Early Years Teachers Attitudes towards Mathematics", M.Ed. dissertation, Centre for Learning Innovation, Faculty of Education, Queensland University of Technology.

Teddlie, Ch. (2005), "Mixed Methods Research Tradition in English", in Encyclopaedia of Educational Administration, Thousand Oaks, California: Sage Publications.

Thurstone L.L. (1931), "The Measurement of Social Attitudes", *Journal of Abnormal and Social Psychology*, 27, pp. 249-269.

White, Pamela, Joy (1997), "The Effects of Teaching Techniques and Teacher Attitudes on Math Anxiety in Secondary Level Students".

Wittrock, M.C. (1986), "Handbook of Research on Teaching, Part 1", American Educational Research Association.

Wood, W. (1982), "Access to Attitude-relevant Information in Memory as a Determinant of Persuasion: The Role of Message Attributes", *Journal of Experimental Social Psychology*, 21, pp. 73-85.

Woolfolk (2003), "Educational Psychology", New York: Sage Publications.

Yesil, H. (2010), "Language Teaching Students Attitude towards Teaching Profession", *International Online Journal of Educational Sciences*, 3(1), pp. 200-219.

Yin, R.K. (1994), "Case Study Research: Design and Methods", second edition, Thousand Oaks, CA: Sage Publications.

Yin, R.K. (2003), "Case Study Research: Design and Methods", third edition, Thousand Oaks, CA: Sage Publications.

Yin, R.K. (2009), "Case Study Research: Design and Methods", fourth edition, Thousand Oaks, CA: Sage Publications.

Index

Index

A
Academic Staff Colleges (ASCs), 133
Adult Education and Lifelong Learning, 20
Adverse Effects of Globalization on Women, 96
Agenda for Sustainable Development, 2
All India Council for Technical Education (AICTE), 133
Apprenticeship Training Scheme (ATS), 127
Aryabhata, 89
Attitude Formation, 64

B
Behaviour of Teacher in a Classroom, 72
Bharat Shiksha Kosh, 102
Bhaskaracharya, 89

C
Central Advisory Board of Education (CABE), 25
Central Board of Secondary Education (CBSE), 118
Central Tibetan Schools (CTSs), 118
Centrally Managed

Schools, 118
Chanakya, 89
Characteristics of Attitude, 59
Cognitive-affective Consistency Theory, 66
Collaborative Teaching, 186
Components of Attitude, 59
Craftsmen Training Scheme (CTS), 127
Curriculum and Pedagogy in Schools, 10

D
Directorate General of Training (DGT), 128
Dissatisfied Teachers, 75
District Primary Education Programme (DPEP), 109

E
Early Childhood Care and Education, 7
Education and Development, 28
Education and Economic Development, 39
Education and Human Potential, 85
Education and Social Development, 38
Education and Women Empowerment, 94

Education for All (EFA), 91

Education Guarantee Scheme and Alternative and Innovative Education (EGS&AIE), 112

Education in Ancient India, 89

Elementary Education Policy, 106

Eleventh Five Year Plan (2007-12), 102

E-Pathshala, 124

Expansion of Higher Education, 131

F

Fundamental Principles of NEP, 2020, 4

G

Gross Domestic Product (GDP), 20

H

Higher Education, 11, 130

Holistic and Multidisciplinary Education, 16

Human Resources and Development, 36

I

Inclusive Education for the Disabled at Secondary Stage (IEDSS), 120

Increase in the Demand for Secondary Education, 115

Information Superhighway, 182

Institutional Development Plan (IDP), 19

Internet and Students, 184

Internet for Research and Academics, 187

J

Jan Shikshan Sansthan, 175

Job-relevant Skills, 154

K

Kasturba Gandhi Balika Vidyalaya Scheme (KGBVS), 109

Kaushal and Rozgar Mela, 171

Kendriya Vidyalayas (KVs), 118

L

Learning Approach, 65

M

Mahila Samakhya, 91

Manpower Planning, 41

Matching Supply of Skills with Demand, 155

Medical Education, 144

Index

Mid-day Meal Schemes, 91

Ministry of Human Resource Development (MHRD), 8

Motivational Theories, 66

N

Narendra Modi, 161, 170

National Apprenticeship Training Scheme (NATS), 172

National Assessment and Accreditation Council (NAAC), 133

National Council for Vocational Training (NCVT), 159

National Council of Educational Research and Training (NCERT), 118

National Education Policy (NEP), 2020, 29, 86

National Educational Technology Forum (NETF), 23

National Institute of Open Schooling (NIOS), 118

National Literacy Mission, 21

National Policy for Skill Development and Entrepreneurship (NPSDE), 2015, 161

National Policy on Education (NPE), 1986, 107

National Programme for Education of Girls at Elementary Level (NPEGEL), 111

National Programme of Nutritional Support to Primary Education (NP-NSPE), 109

National Skill Development Mission (NSDM), 2015, 165

Navodaya Vidyalayas (NVs), 118

O

Objectives of Education Policy, 93

Objectives of Education, 37

Online and Digital Education, 24

On-the-job Training (OJT), 155

Open Distance Learning (ODL), 14

Optimal Learning Environments, 16

P

Placement Guidelines, 171

Plagiarism and Copyright Issues, 189

Pradhan Mantri Gramodaya

Yojana (PMGY), 111
Pradhan Mantri Kaushal Vikas Yojana (PMKVY), 169
Prarambhik Shiksha Kosh (PSK), 112
Private Sector Initiatives for Skill Building, 158
Private Sector Institutions, 146
Professional Education, 20
Promotion of Indian Languages, Arts, and Culture, 101
Public-Private-Partnership in Education, 41

R

Rashtriya Madhyamik Shiksha Abhiyan (RMSA), 119
Rashtriya Uchchatar Shiksha Abhiyan (RUSA), 134
Recruitment and Deployment of Teachers, 103
Right of Children to Free and Compulsory Education (RTE), Act, 2009, 91
Right to Education Act, 9
Role of Education in the Development Process, 91

S

Saakshar Bharat, 176
Samagra Shiksha, 8, 124
Sarva Shiksha Abhiyan (SSA), 108
School Education, 7
Secondary Education Commission, 1953, 117
Self-perception Theory, 66
Shaala Sidhi, 124
Significance of Attitude of Teachers, 57
Skill Development for Women Workers, 160
Special Economic Zones (SEZs), 96
System of Skill Development in India, 157

T

Teacher Eligibility Tests (TETs), 11
Teacher Training and Attitudes, 67
Teachers as Catalysts of Society, 29
Teacher-Student Relationship, 33
Technical Education Institutions in India, 141
Technical Education, 138
Technology and Economic Development, 140

Index 213

Tenth Five Year Plan
    (2002-07), 131
Theories of Attitude
    Formation, 65
Total Literacy Campaign
    (TLC), 174
Trends in Literacy Rates,
    100
Twelfth Five Year Plan
    (2012-17), 89

U
University Grants
    Commission (UGC),
    132
V
Varahamihira, 89
Virtual Library, 189
Vocational Education, 124

W
Wakf Act, 1954, 144
Wireless Application
    Protocol (WAP), 183
Women in Decision-
    making, 99
World Wide Web
    (WWW), 183
World Youth Skills Day,
    166

Z
Zila Saksharata Samities,
    174